To Al,

affectionately,

Anne

The Quiet Profession

The Quiet Profession

Supervisors of Psychotherapy

Anne Alonso, Ph.D.

Assistant Clinical Professor of Psychology
Department of Psychiatry
Harvard Medical School;
Director, Treatment Center
Boston Institute for Psychotherapies
Boston, Massachusetts

Macmillan Publishing Company
New York

Collier Macmillan Canada, Inc.
Toronto

Collier Macmillan Publishers
London

Macmillan Publishing Company
866 Third Avenue, New York, New York 10022

Collier Macmillan Canada, Inc.

Collier Macmillan Publishers • London

Library of Congress Cataloging in Publication Data
Alonso, Anne.
  The quiet profession.

  Bibliography: p.
  Includes index.
  1. Psychotherapy—Study and teaching—Supervision.
2. Psychotherapists—Supervision of. I. Title.
RC480.5.A46 1985   616.89′1′07   83-46129
ISBN 0-02-302300-7

Printing: 1 2 3 4 5 6 7 8   Year: 5 6 7 8 9 0 1 2 3

For Ramón, Marjie, Sarah

Preface

One of the abiding joys of my professional career is the privilege of contributing to the clinical development of psychotherapists from all mental health disciplines. Over the years I have endeavored to understand the supervisory process, and to teach it in a variety of settings. While there are many fine articles and books about supervision, I found myself wishing for a single text that would define the supervisory process and describe its application in a generalizable way. More importantly, it seemed to me that there was a remarkable paucity of attention to the supervisors themselves, and to the normative developmental changes that they experience over the course of their supervisory careers. Thus supervision has been thought of as an addendum to a clinician's work, rather than as a professional subspeciality worthy of distinction. This book is written to remedy that blind spot, and to facilitate the work of supervisors who feel the wish for more clarity around the terrain.

My professional point of view is a psychodynamic one, and the work reflects that bias clearly. However, an attempt is made to address the issues in "plain talk," which I hope is useful to clinicians from a large range of theoretical viewpoints.

In this book, then, the point of view is to focus on the supervisor of psychotherapy, more than on the student in the process. To be sure, I have defined what I mean by supervision, and offered numerous examples to illustrate the process as it is played out between the supervisor and the supervisee, for better and for worse. But the supervisor stands on center stage, as the protagonist of the story, and the focus of our interest and concern.

Acknowledgments

As I try to acknowledge all those who have helped me in this work, the room is filled with memories of past voices ranging back to Sister Victorina, a grade school teacher with a remarkable name and an even more remarkable capacity to inspire, demand, and support; to my own early supervisors, and to my mentors over time. In particular, my students deserve my heartiest thanks for teaching me at least as much as I taught them. Some friends in particular stand out as mainstays in the preparation of this particular work. Drs. Jackie Zilbach, Frederic Hudson, and John Gladfelter made early suggestions and offered inspiration and validation throughout; Drs. J. Scott Rutan, Aaron Lazare, Dan Asnes, and Jerome Gans generously read and critiqued the manuscript, as did Doris Held. My special thanks go to my dear friend and sister, Jean Alonso, for her careful editing and encouragement. Sarah Boardman was especially helpful in shaping and editing the manuscript. Thanks also to Sandy Thompson for typing, posting, and otherwise helping the work along.

My deepest appreciation goes finally to my husband Ramón for his unstinting generosity and patience throughout. Along with our daughters, Marjorie and Sarah, he remains a source of joy and creativity for this and all other work.

Contents

The Quiet Profession

1

Introduction

. . . truth, whose mother is history, who is the rival of time, depository of deeds, witness of the past, example and lesson to the present, and warning to the future. [*Cervantes*, Don Quixote, *Part One, Chap. 9(1)]*

The awesome privilege and the enormous burden of parenting the young come to fruition in the moment when they set forth carrying our visions of the truth and our dreams into posterity. In the complex art of emotional healing that has developed in the last century, a group of professional parents have emerged who have labored to maintain old truths, to communicate them to the present generation, and to enlarge upon them for the future. Psychotherapy supervisors serve as the keepers of the faith, and the mentors of the young. Theirs is a quiet profession that combines the discipline of science with the aesthetic creativity of art. They teach, inspire, cajole, and shape their students toward their own standard of professional excellence. It is a curious paradox that at their best they are the least visible; having set a standard, they provide an intellectual and supportive environ-

3

ment in which a student can ask a question and then answer it for himself.

The primary goal of this book is to validate supervision as a clinical subspeciality, to illuminate the supervisors who practice it, and to establish some guidelines for the development and maintenance of a supervisory career. Psychotherapy supervision is a profession with its own standards, theories, and practitioners who are well identified and legitimized. While supervisors of psychotherapy have long enjoyed a private kind of distinction and respect in the field, they have also labored under an inadequate consciousness of self, with marginal support and approbation for their work. Supervisors need a louder and clearer voice; they need to speak to one another, to train new supervisors into their profession, and to stand apart as specialists who represent a major subspeciality in the clinical field.

The study of supervision stands in sharp contrast to the study of psychotherapy. It is as sparsely documented as the latter is abundantly researched. There continues to be a blindness about the supervisors themselves that parallels some of the earlier and more naive views concerning the importance of the therapist's contribution to the clinical hour. It was thought then that, ideally, the therapist withheld any personal assumptions, biases, and affects from the therapy hour. Countertransference responses were looked at with suspicion as possible indicators of serious problems with the clinician, needing to be resolved in his own therapy and removed from the work with the patient. We have come to revise this view and now respect the clinician's personal reactions as valuable sources of data about the patient and about the therapy. Now it is time to acknowledge the impact of supervisors on the process of clinical training, not only because of the function they provide, but also because, as human beings whose own careers evolve in the course of time, they lend of themselves to the integration of the new clinician's developing professional persona.

Borges (2) describes an emperor who built the Great Wall of China at the same time that he ordered the burning of all the books that had existed before him. If the clinical field is to avoid the trap of ignoring the past as it builds its present structures, the supervisors must be recognized for the vital role they play in carrying the wisdom of the past into the state of the art.

It is intriguing to venture guesses as to why the supervisors have received so little attention in the field of psychotherapy. Several possibilities come to mind, such as automatic adherence to convention, the natural selection of individuals who enter the clinical professions, cultural bias, confusion about role boundaries, and a lack of visibility in the professional community. All are imposing barriers to change. Yet to continue this neglect is to stultify future learning that could enrich our training institutions and add dignity to the profession.

Adherence to convention

Tradition plays a strong role in training institutions. A common response to my questions about the attention to supervisory careers is that we have not done so badly with the present system, so why look for problems where none may exist? This is the usual "good enough for my grandfather" argument, and gives the lie to the basic tenet of psychotherapy, namely that health comes with knowing oneself as fully as possible.

It is true that our training centers are maintained with energy, skill, and goodwill by a large number of fine supervisors whose benevolence and generosity have inspired and trained generations of clinicians; it is also true that their work can be enriched and can be better passed on to their colleagues in a more systematic and lasting way if we dignify it with the careful study it deserves. Even our best supervisors could function more creatively with better theoretical and practical road maps. Furthermore, we need to concern ourselves with enlisting and retaining fine clinicians as supervisors. It has been the tradition that once one finishes being trained as a psychotherapist, one is ready to begin supervising. Many promising supervisors are so disheartened by finding themselves pressed into service with little or no supervisory training that they flee the role and are lost forever to the profession.

Personality characteristics of clinicians

Professional helpers reinforce their self-esteem by helping others. They tend to be uncomfortable with acknowledging their own neediness and vulnerability, focusing instead on meeting the needs of the identified patient or student. Supervisors are not immune to this difficulty, and, in addition, find it awkward to discuss their ignorance with colleagues and to ask for help in what is supposed to be their area of expertise. When this happens their development goes unaided, and they are prone to settle into a static position that may well be adequate, but is deprived of the input that could turn supervision into an exciting professional endeavor.

Another characteristic of professional helpers relates to anxiety about the sadistic instincts stimulated by the power inherent in the role. Committed to a nonjudgmental, healing stance as clinicians, the responsibility of judging the trainee's personal and professional competence is a real departure, and the subsequent discomfort may be difficult to address in public.

Cultural bias

The care-taking and teaching of the young have been identified as a female occupation in western culture, and from this has evolved the subsequent devaluation of those functions and the people who perform them. At the same time, supervisors have enjoyed the status of expert; this cultural split may have contributed to a blind spot about the supervisory role. There is now an excellent opportunity to remedy this defect, given the loosening of gender roles among men and women vis-à-vis the care of the young.

6

The androgynous aspects of supervision are developed in the myth of Mentor, the servant of Odysseus, who is entrusted with the care of his young son, Telemachus. Mentor prepares the boy to succeed his father, but in the latter's absence, the mother's suitors plot to kill the boy and take over the property. At this point, it would seem that the male Mentor can no longer succeed by himself, and Pallas-Athena, the goddess of wisdom, descends to join with Mentor to save the day. She enters his body, and thus, in this merger of male and female personas, they succeed in rescuing Telemachus and sending him off to join his father.

Taken symbolically, we might see the merger of science and art as represented in the two aspects of the effective Mentor, then and now.

Uneasy boundaries

Confusion about supervision extends beyond gender bias into the question of permeable boundaries. Is the supervisor a teacher, a therapist, or some combination of both? Is the supervisor's primary allegiance to the student, to the training institution, or to the patient? It is difficult to be clear about these boundaries for oneself, and even more difficult to teach to a novice.

Another factor that may well have contributed to the silence among supervisors is an appropriate reluctance to discuss peers and future colleagues in the language of clinical pathology. Fortunately, the emergence of the field of adult development has provided us with a viable language for discussing normal oscillations of strength and weakness in a way that applies to a responsible discussion of our trainees.

Professional visibility

The absence of supervisors' professional societies and the scarcity of journals dedicated to publishing research on supervision adds to the overall tendency to ignore the supervisors. In addition, the

7

decreased support for pedagogy in training institutions hardly leaves supervisors in a strong lobbying position. Thus, while they are highly valued in their consultation rooms, there is little mandate or opportunity for them to speak out strongly and publicly for their profession.

In an effort to resolve a blind spot in the mental health field, this book addresses the supervisor of psychotherapy from a variety of perspectives. Chapter Two offers a basic definition of supervision. Chapter Three explores the supervisors in terms of who they are, and why they do what they do. Chapter Four defines what they do, and Chapter Five explores how they evolve over the life span, both as human beings and as supervisors. Chapter Six describes supervisory impasse, elaborates the supervisor's positive and negative influence on the impasse, and gives several examples of impasse resolution. Chapter Seven discusses innovations in supervision. Chapter Eight is an anatomy of a supervision, and Chapter Nine suggests some models for the training of supervisors.

We stand at the beginning of an important dialogue that has major implications for serious clinicians from all mental health disciplines. Careful study of supervisors and supervision is in its infancy. We need ways to conduct outcome research on supervision, to develop theory of supervision, and to create an exciting climate of enquiry around the whole endeavor. Just as no person can enjoy self-esteem until he can find it in himself to take pride in some aspects of his lineage, so no profession can fulfill its ideals until it honors those who have contributed to its continuity and to its present state of richness.

References

1. Cervantes, M. de, *Don Quixote*, Chap. 9, Part 1, 1605, trans. by Walter Starkey, London, MacMillan, 1957, p. 109.
2. Borges, J. L., *Other Inquisitions*, 1937–1952, N.Y.: Washington Square Press, Inc., 1966, pp. 1–4.

2

What Is Supervision?

It is as difficult to define supervision as it is to define psychotherapy. Freud argued that psychoanalysis is a cure through love. Others insist it is a scientific method. Both positions seem grossly inadequate to define such a complex human process as exists between patient and therapist. Efforts to define supervision founder on similar shoals, ranging from abstract but amorphous to concrete but overly restricting definitions.

This chapter begins with a general definition of supervision that is widely accepted. Other definitions that tend to focus more particularly on one aspect or another of the supervisory process slant the definition in the direction of the definer's primary emphasis for the work, and are therefore controversial. Nonetheless, each elaborates some important aspects of the work, and some integration of these enriches our knowledge of the supervisory scope. Summed up, there are three major viewpoints that exist in the clinical literature and we will examine these as well.

A general definition

Supervision is the primary professional training model for mental health clinicians. It involves four distinct entities: the patient, the therapist-in-training, the supervisor, and the administration of the training institution. At its best it is a situation in which the administration is charged with creating and maintaining a clinical environment in which all can grow and flourish, and the supervisor is fully committed to the development of the neophyte clinician. This leaves the clinician in charge of the patient.

Each party brings to the interaction particular concerns, but when the work is going well, these varied concerns are balanced in a synchronous range of interests, and are fulfilling to everyone. The patient works toward health; the trainee/therapist works toward the health of the patient and toward his own clinical development. The administration safeguards the well-being of all and the public's ethical and mental health standards. The supervisor is sensitive to the needs of all parties, and takes any measures necessary for the responsible and ethical/legal care of the patient's safety, while making his primary responsibility the training of the young clinician.

For the sake of our ensuing discussion, let us create an example of this four-part system of administration, supervisor, therapist-in-training, and patient.

> *EXAMPLE:* Boston General Hospital employs Dr. Sears to oversee the work of Dr. Young, who is treating Mr. Prout. The dynamic process between them optimally is balanced and mutually satisfactory. The balance inevitably shifts from time to time, however, and part of the supervisor's task is to employ his skill to restore this balance. If Mr. Prout, for example, becomes acutely suicidal, Dr. Sears will shift his attention more toward the patient, a move he would want to avoid in the normal course of events. This temporary shift may even be to the point of overruling Dr. Young's decisions, and perhaps compromising some level of his learning. Similarly, should the

administration be dissatisfied with Dr. Young's work, they may request reports or activities on the supervisor's part that may result in some curtailment of Dr. Young's progress in the profession; such a move would again pull Dr. Sears away from his usual priorities of concern for his supervisee.

Any of these choices may generate a set of reactions in Dr. Sears that have only indirectly to do with the case at hand. He may recall a patient of his who committed suicide and become so invested in protecting Mr. Prout that he essentially takes over the case inappropriately. Or he may harbor some negative feeling toward the administration that would make it difficult for him to participate in resolving the training conflict with an adequate measure of objectivity and calm. Or he may over-identify with Dr. Young because he reminds him of his own son; this may lead him to distort the real needs of the trainee or of the training institution.

The situation described in this example is not so unusual. It is part and parcel of the everyday interaction in any training institute. Its complexity serves to clarify the magnitude of the supervisor's contribution, and emphasizes the need for the highly professional quality of his involvement and influence.

To steer the course of the supervisory process, the supervisor needs a set of assumptions and methods to bring about change. The formal study of these—the literature on supervision of psychotherapy—dates to the early 1920s, at the Berlin Psychoanalytic Institute. In the main, the literature divides into three major categories. Supervision is seen as: (1) a cognitive and primarily didactic process; (2) an emotional growth experience for the maturing clinician; and (3) an interpersonal process that focuses on the empathic connectedness between the concerned parties. The latter view tends to stand in the middle ground between the other two. Both kinds of learning are emphasized, with the overall goal of helping the trainee to enter the patient's experience and to know his world from within, as much as is humanly possible.

The cognitive definition

A major function of supervision is to teach. According to the Oxford English Dictionary, to teach is to show by way of information.* In the cognitive model of supervision the student is expected to learn the theory of psychology and psychotherapy, to study technique of assessment, diagnosis, treatment of mental disorders, and to conduct research into these areas. It is the supervisor's task to transmit the information, to follow the progress of the trainee's work, to check up on both errors and new developments in learning, and finally, to assess and evaluate whether the student has adequately garnered and integrated the information so that he or she can function as an independent practitioner without the need for further supervision.

Proponents of this view see teaching as a hierarchical structure with the teacher as the source of data, and the student as a somewhat passive recipient of the new information. The student as passive learner is consistent with this philosophy of hierarchical teaching. Initially the transfer of information from the supervisor down to the student is the model that holds. Of course, the student is expected eventually to relinquish passivity and integrate the data. Two clear proponents of this view are Tarachow (1) and Langs (2). They stress the necessity to avoid infantilizing the learner, which they see as a hazard specific to this philosophy of supervising, wherein the student is clearly defined as the recipient of wisdom and direction. Specifically, they propose that supervision stay strictly focused on the treatment of the patient and avoid any discussion of the clinician's personal needs in learning except as they are directly relevant to the case at hand. While clearly sensitive to the involvement of the clinician's personality factors in the supervisory work, they insist that the cognitive task is primary.

There is some variation among thinkers in this category. The concept of androgogy, or adult learning, is proposed by Knowles

---

*As distinct from Dewey's definition of learning by doing, for example.

(3). The term refers specifically to adult education, as opposed to pedagogy, or the education of children. They resist the hierarchical model for adult learners. Mutual learning is emphasized as a very important and valued aspect of an androgogical situation. Nonetheless, the cognitive accumulation and integration of facts remains the main thrust of the concern of this group. The facts are both objective and subjective. The external realities of the patient's history and symptom picture are collected, along with the fantasies and feelings of both the patient and therapist.

Implicit in this definition are certain very important statements about the supervisor/trainee relationship. First, objective data collection and assessment should be independent of personality variables. Any supervisor of comparable skill should be able to initiate, take over, or evaluate the work of any given trainee. Essentially, the supervisors are interchangeable in this relationship.

Also, any difficulties in the supervisory situation can be understood as a problem of insufficient data due to incomplete or poor teaching, or as an inability on the part of the trainee to understand, recall, or apply theory to technique, and so forth. It follows that more teaching should improve the situation, given adequate intelligence, mental health, and motivation on the trainee's part. This cognitive view of supervision as teaching represents one end of the spectrum as defined by the majority of supervisors. While no one would dispute that supervisors must teach, this seems a surprisingly narrow view for psychotherapists, whose major emphasis is often on the importance of non-cognitive, out-of-awareness impediments to growth, development, and learning. These positions tend to be ones of major rather than exclusive focus, and in practice, most supervisors employ some measure of all positions.

Let us return to our example and examine some specific interventions that a primarily cognitive supervisor would be apt to make:

Dr. Young presents his concerns with Mr. Prout's expression of despair for the future. Here, Dr. Sears would probably begin teaching by asking some very specific questions about the important variables that contribute to levels of suicidal risk—e.g., the patient's prior history with suicidal behavior, family history of suicide, and the specificity of the patient's plan for suicide. (In fact, every responsible supervisor is sure to do this preliminary assessment of safety and risk.) The next responses are those that are representative of the cognitive position. Dr. Sears would refer Dr. Young to the clinical literature on mourning and melancholia, or to other theoretical writings about depression and suicide; he would teach him to scan the patient's earlier hours for data that would explain his increased distress, focusing on signs of regression in the patient, or hints of previously undetected symptoms, such as early morning awakening, or weight loss; he would then discuss the various options available, such as increasing the frequency of contact, or adding psychopharmacologic treatment; consider the pros and cons of hospitalization, or doing nothing; discuss the inevitability of periodic regression and its meaning in the normal course of treatment with this kind of patient; advise Dr. Young of the legal and ethical measures for which he is responsible, and assure that the records in the case are up-to-date and accurate. In all likelihood, he would discuss with the trainee the advisability of alerting the administrative chief of the service should the risk be significant.

Dr. Sears, meanwhile, would be observing Dr. Young's personal level of anxiety and confusion and his overall competence. In this model, these would not be discussed openly, but would be registered by the supervisor in terms of understanding and helping his student. They would focus instead on Mr. Prout's progress or lack of it in this hour, and how it ties in with his history and prognosis, while relating the situation to the appropriate theory of psychopathology. In sum, Dr. Sears' interventions are mostly directed to the intellectual grasp of the clinical situation by Dr. Young with Mr. Prout as the exclusive focus of concern. Objective criteria, theory, and plans of action constitute the content of the supervision; the process is primarily focused on the conscious, manifest levels of Mr. Prout's dialogue with his therapist, and his interactions with his world outside the hour.

The emotional definition

At the other end of the spectrum are those supervisors who assume that the development of a clinician from novice to expert is primarily an emotional, maturational process, much like the development of a child from infancy to adulthood.

It is imperative here that the supervisee be nourished with theoretical depth and personal therapy, and be housed in a protective training environment. Beyond these givens, maturity and fruition will grow from attention to the novice's increasing capacity to develop a positive sense of his professional self. The trainee becomes more like a patient than like a student. For example, in most training centers for psychoanalysis, the supervisor is seen as a therapist/mentor of sorts, who oversees the work of the trainee with a specific eye to the personality of the trainee and the ways that his internal life may be adding to or distracting from the work with the patient. The acquisition of theory and objective facts pertaining to clinical practice are expected to occur in seminars or elsewhere.

Most proponents of this view (4–6) still distinguish between therapy or analysis, and supervision. Psychotherapy, especially psychodynamic psychotherapy, is a process of inviting regression in the service of emotional growth. Supervision, on the other hand, is distinguished from psychotherapy in its process and in its goals. It is assumed that a transference relationship will develop between therapist and supervisor and that this transferential field will become a primary vehicle for influencing the student's clinical growth. For the purposes of supervision the training situation is regressive enough. The emphasis is on progressive rather than regressive movement; there is a concerted effort to shore up and strengthen the supervisee's healthiest defenses, either by reducing the ambiguity or by helping the trainee to tolerate the inevitable confusion of clinical work. It is assumed that the trainee is in treatment so that undue distress catalyzed by the work with the patients will be handled in that arena. The supervisor presumes that the student is an adult with good levels of self-esteem, who has clear ego boundaries and is capable of handling intimate relationships. When difficulty occurs in these spheres in the course of the clinical work, this regression is seen as a healthy and expectable rite of passage through which one moves from novice to mature psychotherapist (7,8). With encouragement and support, the trainee is expected to reconstitute to prior levels of competence. In fact, the clinician who never regresses in the course of training is probably avoiding the more difficult levels of learning that occur in the unconscious merger of patient/therapist and may be keeping too great a distance between self and patient.

In the theory of emotional growth, the supervisor is seen as playing a highly personal role in the training of the young clinician, and is not the interchangeable supervisor outlined in the cognitive definition. The emphasis on the emotional development of the clinician implies strongly that the relationship with the supervisor is integrally woven into the clinician's future development. The supervisory relationship defined here is an intimate one, in which both parties invest in a mutual exploration of less conscious processes, and in which both parties experience growth and tension. Searles (9) is eloquent in his argument that the supervisor and the student are engaged in a similar process of helping each other to mutually develop through the synergy of their relationship.

To return to our example, if Dr. Sears is to supervise from this perspective, he would probably begin with the same safety measures but then would move to the effects of Mr. Prout's communication with regard to suicide on Dr. Young. Similarly, he would be wondering about which conflicts Dr. Young may have contributed to this dilemma, or for that matter, which aspects of the supervisory relationship may have played a part as well. In other words he would focus on transference and countertransference impulses that may be distorting the work.

Obviously he would have to exercise tact and respect the timing of any overt explorations of these factors, but whether or not he discussed them overtly with Dr. Young, they would constitute a major focus of his attention. He might do any or all of the following: Help Dr. Young become aware of his own anxiety, or rage, or affection for the patient, which are below the level of awareness in the young clinician, but which might be clouding his vision of the case; Discuss the effects of "helplessness in the helpers" (10). In addition to sharing theory, he might offer examples from his own clinical work to the student, in which even a senior supervisor is prone to feel frustrated and despairing with certain patients, or in particular kinds of clinical crises; Alert Dr. Young to attend to his dreams and fantasies about the patient; Consider the treatment options both objectively and subjectively, i.e., what to do, and how will it feel to both the therapist and the patient to pursue such a course.

Should Dr. Young prove to be very upset, Dr. Sears might suggest that Dr. Young bring up the situation in his own therapy. He might also express some support for the ultimate value of this kind of personal "overinvestment" in the early clinical work, with a goal of reducing the shame and anxiety that the trainee might otherwise experience if told to take up training issues in his treatment.

The supervisor in this model is clearly focused on the clinician first, and on the patient secondarily. He is interested in the expanding of Dr. Young's clinical capacity with this and any other patient, and uses the case at hand as an opportunity to help the trainee to fine tune himself as the instrument of the clinical work for this and future cases. He pays direct attention to the emotional field between clinician, patient, and himself, and directs the student to attend to his internal clues. He offers himself as a model for this kind of exploration of the less rational, more emotional clinical responses—the countertransference aspects of the work. Just as importantly, he remains alert to his own counter-reactions to the supervisory situation, and looks to these first when the work gets difficult.

Most supervisors seem to function between the two poles described above. Primary among this group are Ekstein and Wallerstein (11) and Semrad (12). Supervision is often described in this middle ground as not quite teaching, but not quite therapy. Fleming and Benedek (13) refer to this as "syncretic dilemma." The supervisor acts in the capacity of a mentor—a trusted friend and counsellor—teaching a baseline of theoretical knowledge, guiding the practice of techniques wherein theory is applied, and supporting the young clinician in the development of empathy, and in the capacity to bear the ambiguity and intense, often frightening material of the therapeutic process. The mentor acts as a model, sharing attitudes, experiences, perspectives, moral, ethical, and practical positions vis-à-vis patients and others in positions of diminished power and authority. Like Mentor with Telemachus, the supervisor guides the trainee without overprotecting or controlling. He encourages moderate levels of risk-taking and creativity, but in the safe context of stable amounts of basic security for all parties to the interaction. Security is achieved by continued attention to the internal and external stresses on the trainee, and by the clear availability of the supervisor as an empathic counsellor in all aspects of the work.

Supervisors of this school rely heavily on attention to the "parallel process" (14) that occurs when the student is trustingly allied with the supervisor. This parallel process is a situation of limited transference that develops in the context of a learning alliance where the therapist feels safe and respected. The therapist unconsciously selects from the plethora of patient material those process issues of conflict for both the patient and the therapist. The trainee then presents these processes either directly, or indirectly by creating the attitudes, affects, or dilemmas that replicate those in the therapy hour with the patient. There is an unconscious wish that the supervisor will heal both the therapist and the patient. The supervisor then can respond to the trainee in terms of the patient's needs, aware that both the student and the patient are the targets of the supervisory communication.

In our model, when Dr. Young presents his concerns about Mr. Prout's increasing despair to the mentor, Dr. Sears is careful to take into account the following factors in determining how he will supervise the situation. He might begin by checking his own level of anxiety or discouragement about the case. Is the therapist making him feel as despairing as the patient is making the trainee feel, or is the despair in the patient alone? If the former is true, then the supervisor may take this opportunity to share with the clinician his own responses to certain clinical situations that make him feel helpless, full of rage, despairing. He might want to give the trainee the opportunity to express other more shameful affects that he may be experiencing toward the patient, such as rage, boredom, or scorn by explaining to the trainee that these are probably induced by the limited merger with the patient, and by teaching the student to value these clues as important data about the patient. He might look into the personality and life stage similarity between the patient and the doctor. He can increase accurate empathy by emphasizing differences if the therapist feels too merged for comfort, or similarities if the therapist is taking a defensively distant stance. He may discuss the treatment options, giving examples from his own clinical experience to elaborate a range of scenarios. In so doing, his primary goal would be to lend himself to the therapist as a role model, and invite identification with a competent senior clinician as an alternative to an over-identification with a vulnerable patient. If Dr. Sears thinks that his personality and Dr. Young's are an awkward match, such as to preclude identification, he might suggest that the student also discuss the case with another supervisor who is closer in style or temperament to Dr. Young. He may review Dr. Young's caseload and protect the supervisee from an overload of too many similar patients at any one point in time. In particular, he may request that the student be assigned a particular kind of patient with whom he might feel more competent so that he can experience some success in another arena.

Factors that determine the choice of a supervisory model

A number of variables determine what kind of supervision is utilized. A major one is the memory of the supervisor's own training experience, and his recall of the best and worst supervisors to whom he was exposed. In the absence of more formal training in supervision, imitation is often the most powerful resource the supervisor has to call upon. Another has to do with the personality preference of the supervisor, coupled with his age and gender, and the developmental imperatives that accompany these variables. This aspect will be examined at length in Chapter Five. The setting for supervision is a major determinant in a number of ways: the philosophy of treatment espoused by the administration, and the specific needs of the patient population are two major variables that influence the direction of the work. For example, in most prepaid health plans, the commitment to short-term therapy dictates the direction of the supervision; in some community mental health clinics, there is often a press to intervene actively and on many fronts in the patients' lives, and this activist approach may put a lot of pressure on the supervisor to be similarly active in the work of supervision with the trainee.

This brings us finally to the trainee, whose level of experience must be taken into account in terms of how much can be assumed to have been acquired elsewhere. Just as in therapy the clinician must meet the patient's level of awareness in the beginning, so must the supervisor make a careful assessment of the supervisor's internal and external realities in order to form a learning alliance that can support the work of clinical training. Semrad even goes so far as to recommend a learning diagnosis of the trainee (15). This "diagnosis" should take into account the realistic assessment of the student's learning style, present level of sophistication in terms of theory and technique, and those aspects of the student's personality that can predict his/her particular strengths and vulnerabilities in the learning situation.

Having delineated a general frame of reference and definition of supervision, we can now turn to our study of the quiet player in the system—the agent who in fact defines, models, and negotiates the dynamic process—the supervisor. Who, typically, are the supervisors? What are some common characteristics and factors in their supervisory experience? What motivates them to supervise? What are the most important functions of the supervisor, and what are the developmental stages in the profession and the person of the supervisor that play a part in shaping the supervisory process itself?

Thus far, this chapter has been concerned with the definitions of supervision as serving the needs of the administration, the therapist, and the patient. In addition, supervision serves some very significant purposes that are in the interest of the supervisor, and this book concerns itself primarily with studying the supervisor. Every supervisor has a plenitude of professional and personal developmental issues that are served by the process; a thorough study of supervision cannot ignore the interests of the supervisor as an integral party to the training system.

References

1. Tarachow, S. *An Introduction to Psychotherapy.* New York: International University Press, 1963.
2. Langs, R. *The Supervisory Experience.* New York: Jason Aronson, 1979.
3. Knowles, M. S. *The Modern Practice of Adult Education: Androgogy vs. Pedagogy.* New York: Association Press, 1970.
4. Limentani, A. The training analyst and the difficulties in the training psychoanalytic situation. *Int. J. Psychoanal.* 3(1): 55–71, 1974.
5. Fleming, H., & Benedek, T. *Psychoanalytic Supervision.* New York: Grune & Stratton, 1966.
6. Aarons, Z. A. The application of psychoanalysis to psychiatric training. *Int. J. Psychiatry* 3(2): 178–203, 1974.
7. Rice, C., Alonso, A., Rutan, J. The fights of spring: separation, individuation and grief in training centers. In *Psychotherapy* 22(7): 97–100, 1985.
8. Shershow, J., & Savodnik, I. Regression in the service of residency education. *Arch. Cen. Psychiatry* 33(10): 1266–70, 1976.
9. Searles, H. Problems of psychoanalytic supervision (1962) in *Collected Papers on Schizophrenia and Related Subjects.* New York: International Universities Press, 1965.
10. Adler, G. Helplessness in the Helpers. *British Journal of Med. Psychology,* 1972.

11. Ekstein, R., Wallerstein, R. *The Teaching and Learning of Psychotherapy.* New York: Basic Books, 1963.
12. Semrad, E. *Teaching Psychotherapy of Psychotic Patients.* New York: Grune & Stratton, 1969.
13. Fleming, H. and Benedek, T., *op. cit.*
14. Ekstein, R. and Wallerstein, R., *op. cit.*
15. Semrad, E. *op. cit.*

3

Who Are the Supervisors?

Supervisors constitute an elite group of teacher/mentors who are valued and honored for their impact on the future of the clinical field. That their prestige and recognition are subtle is consistent with the overall quiet that surrounds the supervisory aspect of the clinical system.

To utilize the strengths of a system fully, it is imperative that all its parts be understood clearly. For this reason it behooves us to bring the supervisor out of the shadow and illuminate the person, his professional situation, and the motivations that lie behind the choice of that career.

A cross-sectional profile of supervisors from all disciplines shows a number of characteristics which, taken as a whole, point to high levels of dedication and altruism. Supervisors are considered experts in their field. They are looked upon with admiration and respect by students and colleagues. They earn this respect by putting their professional acumen on the line in a variety of ways. They are expected to remain current in the professional literature; they regularly voice their clinical opinions and judgments, and defend them to students and sometimes to the administration as well. They share the legal liability in the cases they supervise. They accept the high demands for vigilance their trainee's work and in their own; they are often confronted with and their student's errors, and with their own, and must publicly acknowledge these errors. This willingness to leave the security of the private consultation room places them in the public eye as the standard bearers of the profession. It is they who set the baseline for what will be considered prudent, ethical, and professional practice in the day-to-day work with patients.

Supervisors enjoy a whole range of personal benefits beyond status and respect. In itself the opportunity to exercise altruism is a healing and generative process. In addition, there is often an academic appointment attached to a supervisory position, bringing a host of options for supervisors with more scholarly interests. These options include an opportunity to engage in professional dialogue with colleagues, to find partners for professional writing and clinical research, to teach, and to attend professional lecture series.

In the context of the current emphasis on pathological narcissism, it is all too easy to overlook elements of healthy narcissistic development. Everyone needs to be admired, loved, sought after, validated, and even feared. Clinicians in isolated private practice run the risk of overdependency on their patients for the satisfaction of these needs, especially at times of distress in their personal lives. Freud, in his letters to Fleiss (1), envied his friend the opportunity to work in the sun, rather than in the shade—in the light of conscious interactions rather than in the murky dark of the unconscious. In supervision, the supervisor is free to deal with only the conscious level of communication, without the burden of always needing to interpret the unconscious aspect of meaning. Although supervisees are just as much in want of tactful and measured responses, there is more room for error, as well as room for direct expression of feeling that the supervisor would not feel justified in expressing with patients. It it perhaps this opportunity to be more "natural" and spontaneous with students than it is appropriate to be with patients that supervisors cherish most. This loosening of the strict vigilance and self-denial does much to avoid the "burn-out" phenomena that has been described in those settings where the work is unremittingly stressful to the clinicians.

And ultimately, most supervise because it is fun. It is exciting to make order out of chaos, to see one's efforts come to fruition in the growth and development of the novice therapist's competence. Supervisors tend to be aware of the wish to pass on the torch through their trainees, and to have a memorable, benign influence on the future of their profession. One's supervisees are often perceived as a ticket to posterity.

In addition to the benefits, a number of factors intrinsic to supervision in the 1980s have the potential to confuse or distort the supervisory role. Some have to do with the role itself, some with the context in which supervision is practiced.

Complexities stemming from the supervisory role

Donald Winnicott has described the concept of good-enough parenting (2), which has direct application to the supervision of psychotherapy. Just as people of a wide variety of personality types and caretaking styles can be good-enough parents, so can a wide range of supervisors be good enough.

One's supervisory role is determined by conscious elements, such as theoretical choice and learned technique, and in part by unconscious factors. The latter include unresolved conflicts that originate in the supervisor's early life, the imperatives of his current stage of adult development, and overall life experiences that may contribute to blind spots such as age and gender bias.

All these elements shape the mentor and contribute unique perspectives for the young clinician, as we shall see in later chapters. This subjectivity, however, can lead trainees to complain loudly about confusion when two supervisors present apparently polar opposite views of the same patient hour or very different judgments about the young clinician's work. Their perception of the differences is very real, as illustrated in the following example: While extreme, it illustrates the dilemma clearly.

EXAMPLE: Five supervisors who had attended the same grand rounds at a major teaching hospital were asked what they thought of the presenter and of his work. They responded as follows:

S.1: "A brilliant and articulate young man. He'll be a big name in the field some day."

S.2: "He has no heart, is the trouble!"

S.3: "Hasn't he come a long way! He used to be impossible in the emergency service."

S.4: "Not bad, not great. They all sound the same after a while."

S.5: "This is an inappropriate case for psychodynamic psychotherapy, so no wonder it's so hard to understand the presenter."

Each supervisor is obviously responding to a different aspect of the work, and with highly idiosyncratic judgments. There is, in fact, no one correct formula by which to treat a patient or to supervise or judge a clinician. Supervision might better be thought of as a mutual learning process, a collaboration between the supervisor and therapist to stretch and adapt to and enlighten one another. Given a wide variety of supervisors in the course of training, the clinician will have opportunities to assimilate and integrate aspects of many styles into a personally congruent identity as a mature clinician.

The awareness of this subjectivity allows the supervisor to help the student tolerate the confusion, especially if the supervisor can negotiate a reasonable position between a clearly articulated and committed stand, on the one hand, and an ability to keep an open mind that does not preclude new learning or an expansion of his clinical horizons.

Complexities that arise from the context

The institutional context in which the supervisor works influences the shape of the work, and is both a spur to creativity and a limiting factor. Some of the institutional constraints have to do with the sometimes confusing reality that supervisors owe fealty to their employers as well as to their supervisees. In fact, some writers define the supervisory job as primarily an administrative one (3,4). If the training environment is healthy and communication is clear and honest at all levels, this mixed loyalty presents no real problems. In fact, the supervisor is in an ideal position to help negotiate mutually creative goals between administration and trainees, since he is aware of the strengths and vulnerabilities of both. For example, a supervisor might help place a supervisee who needs more clinical experience with psychotic patients in an in-patient setting, or might assure that the next rotation includes work with a supervisor who is expert in the care of such patients.

All of this requires that the supervisor respect the goals of the institution, as well as those of the students and see them as mutually achievable. Only then can he maintain with integrity and enthusiasm the role of a two-way conduit and guide.

Where the supervisor does not respect the system or feels bored or devalued by it, then the supervisory process is likely to be compromised. A notable example of this sort of impasse occurred in the wake of President Lyndon Johnson's failed war on poverty in the 1970s, when mental health clinics and training institutions began to experience severe financial constraints and greater cost-accountability. In the reorganization toward a fee-for-service atmosphere, many supervisors experienced a sharp diminution of flexible time that had long been one of the benefits of holding supervisory positions; this "perk" had allowed them to write, to conduct research, and to spend time with colleagues in clinical and theoretical discussions. Feeling disrespected by the system and deprived by the new time charts, they were prone to experience a diminished self-esteem about their supervisory identities. Those systems that were sensitive to this dilemma sought to affirm the value of their supervisors by including them in continuing education efforts, or by inviting them to participate in departmental functions and committees, but the shock waves of the contraction of training funds have left most training institutions with much reduced and straightened fiscal resources.

The involvement of third-party providers in the delivery of mental health care has generated some awkward moves by a large number of mental health clinics seeking to comply with additional requirements at a time of reduced resources. This affects the supervisory system in a variety of ways. Often providers require a specified number of supervisors for each deliverer of care; thus, if, as is often the case, many of the staff are very young, they will be pressed into supervising students long before they feel ready to do so. For them, and often for their students, supervision becomes an anxiety-laden situation in which both feel equally threatened, and may feel equally tempted to avoid. This is a truly unfortunate situation since many clinicians who might have become excellent supervisors flee from the role after such a premature experience.

For all of its complexity, the supervisory role is a fulfilling one; that it is seen as desirable is evidenced by the fact that the finest clinician/mentors in a system are prepared to supervise for little or no financial remuneration, and to enter into the complexities with energy and creativity year after year. It is clear that the primary motivation is the love of the work itself, as alluded to by Erik Erikson:

> Man needs to teach, not only for the sake of those who need to be taught, and not only for the fulfillment of his identity, but because facts are kept alive by being told, logic by being demonstrated, truth by being professed. . . . Every mature adult knows the satisfaction of explaining what is dear to him and of being understood by a groping mind. Care is the widening concern for what has been generated by love, necessity, or accident; it overcomes the ambivalence adhering to irreversible obligation (5).

References

1. Freud, S. Letters to Fleiss, #84 (March 10, 1898) Standard Edition, Vol. I, p. 274.
2. Winnicott, D. *Collected Papers.* New York: Basic Books, 1958.
3. Scherz, F. H. A concept of supervisor based on definitions of job responsibility. *Social Casework* XXXIV: 435, 1958.

4. Kaslow, F., & Associates. Supervision, *Consultation and Staff Training in the Helping Professions*. San Francisco: Jossey-Bass, Inc., 1978.

5. Erikson, E. *Insight and Responsibility*. New York: W. W. Norton Co., Inc., 1964, p. 13.

4

What Do Supervisors Do?

Supervisors perform a large number of complex acitivities that range along a continuum from didactic teaching, to interpersonal influence, to administrative intervention, to metatherapy.

This chapter examines supervisory functions by separating them for heuristic purposes. In fact, they all occur simultaneously, with greater or lesser emphasis depending on the particular style of a given supervisor, or the needs of the student. For example, in the first year of training, a student may require large amounts of information, so the supervisor may rely a great deal on didactic teaching of theory and technique; he may want to provide positive support, and avoid negative criticism in this narcissistically vulnerable stage of training. By the third year of training, the supervisor might want to focus on helping him to elicit the patient's transference, to attend to his own countertransferential response, and to respond appropriately.

The setting of supervision also influences the work. In an emergency room setting, the supervisor is much more apt to be directive than in the calm of an outpatient practice, where the fine points of psychotherapy can be attended to without fear for the safety of the patient.

A. Didactic teaching.

Teaching is universally accepted as the primary function of a supervisor. First of all, the supervisor must *teach some fundamental clinical methods and procedures,* and their theoretical bases. This means for example, that the student/therapist must learn why and whether to answer a patient's question, and how this decision relates to the theoretical underpinnings of the technique. If the theoretical baseline is psychodynamic, the response will probably differ quite a bit from that of the behaviorist or the counselor. This applied teaching is usually left to the supervisor, and undertaken didactically for the most part.

In addition, the supervisor teaches the clinician to *hear subtleties in the patient's communications,* at the level of the manifest as well as the latent dimensions. This kind of "listening with the third ear" (1) requires equal attention to the process of the communication—(why is the patient saying this now, in this way?)—as well as to the content of what the patient is saying, and its very particular meaning to this patient.

Further, the supervisor teaches how to *gather data* about the patient, *to listen in an organized way,* and *to create decision trees* that will allow for orderly thinking about the case at hand. The direction of treatment requires that the clinician adequately *diagnose, formulate,* and derive some *idea of prognosis of treatment.* The supervisor teaches the clinician how to organize all the data from the patient, how to arrive at a diagnosis, and how to formulate the case. This formulation will allow the student to plot the course of treatment, to learn what can be expected given a particular patient's goals and capacities, and to gauge how to assess objectively the appropriate time to end treatment. The clinician *must map out a treatment plan* that meets the needs of the patient within the available options for that patient, and within the capacity of the clinician to deliver. *How to seek con-*

sultation, how to decide whether to refer to another treatment modality or to another clinician, or even when *to decide that treatment is not appropriate*—all these are crucial skills that are learned optimally in the supervisory hour.

B. Imparting an appropriate attitude toward patients

In this aspect of the work, which is sometimes thought of as the art of supervision, the nature of supervising shifts, becoming subtler and calling on skills beyond the didactic. The supervisor teaches and models *an attitude of open-minded curiosity combined with a nonjudgmental stance* that reassures all parties that nothing is forbidden or dangerous to talk about. The growing ability to feel and communicate respect for even the most difficult patient is a major hallmark of a maturing clinician. The student further needs to learn *how to maintain an attitude of hovering attention* that listens both to the patient and to the clinician's own internal response simultaneously, however uncomfortable the latter may be. For example, if a patient is acting very compliant, and profusely thanking the clinician, while the clinician feels anxious and worried about the lack of progress in the patient's life, the crossed signals must be examined with an eye to understanding whether the patient is dissimulating or whether the doctor is worried that a beloved patient may terminate and leave him behind!

C. Expanding the affective capacity of the therapist

Generally speaking the new clinician begins with a limited set of emotional experiences and unlimited good will and eagerness to be of help to the patient. To become a professional therapist the student must *complement this kind of sympathetic outlook with the capacity to deliberately feel and contain intense and primitive feelings*. In so doing, it then becomes possible to experience the world from the context of even the most disturbed patient—

39

in short, to *empathize** with a wide range of human dilemmas and affects.

The supervisor needs first to make an empathic diagnosis (2) of the student, i.e., to experience the clinicial hour that is presented in supervision from within the student's context. In what areas is the student empathically in tune with the patient, and in what areas is he out of empathy? How much of the lack of empathy is related to the student's naiveté about the patient's dilemma, and to what extent is it a defence from threatening affects? The supervisor is called upon to show high levels of acceptance and tactful intervention aimed at helping the student to "stretch" empathic boundaries, and to serve as a safe container even for the patient's most regressed expressions of feeling.

In order for the clinician to stretch emotional boundaries, he must learn to *accept a sense of ambiguity* about the work and be willing to be led by the patient into unfamiliar territory. This ambiguity can be very painful for the novice who, feeling largely ignorant in any case, may be eager to get intellectual closure on an idea or a situation in order to feel more secure and helpful. In addition, the vagueness around emotionally-charged material catalyzes anxiety and regression in the therapist. This kind of emotional overload can complicate things even further by making it difficult for the therapist to present a well-formulated hour to the supervisor. It is here that the experience with the supervisor will lead to increased empathy for patients. If the supervisor can be inviting and nonjudgmental about the clinician's feelings and fantasies about the case, if he can contain and work with intense feelings between the self and the therapist that arise in the supervisory hour, if he can hear the clinician's anger about the training institution without judging or colluding, then the student learns how to do the same with the patient. No amount of didactic teaching can replace the value of the experiential

*Empathy here is defined as a capacity to fuse temporarily with another, and to experience that person's world from within his own frame of reference. This is only possible when the person empathizing is clear and secure about ego boundaries, and knows that the fusion is temporary and can be terminated at will.

learning that occurs in supervision about these aspects of the training. Similar learning occurs with regard to the tolerance of ambiguity if the supervisor freely admits ignorance, and avoids appearing wise and certain in a situation which in fact leaves him unsure and perplexed (3). Searles (4) describes the supervisor as needing to tolerate ambiguity and exclusion from the therapist/patient symbiosis and points out that he must also avoid sadistic intrusions stemming from a sense of uselessness and object hunger. Searles is referring to the fact that supervisors commonly feel left out of an inviting intimacy between the patient and the therapist. At such times, the supervisor may intrude unnecessarily into the material in order to feel he is making an impact. Sometimes these intrusions are subtle, and take the form of asking for more details, or making gratuitous suggestions, or taking much too vigilant a stance toward the therapist's work. This kind of supervisory maneuver can undermine the therapist's confidence, and leave him feeling more dependent on the supervisor.

D. Developing the capacity to work in the metaphor of the transference

Transference is defined here as the unconscious distortion of the present due to interference from unresolved past conflicts. These conflicts are invited to surface from repression by the heated emotional climate of the hour, and their interpretation is seen by psychodynamic clinicians as a major avenue for change. Freud states "The peculiarity of the transference to the physician lies in its excess, in both character and degree, of what is rational and justifiable" (5). Encouragement of this kind of excessive response in the patient is difficult to achieve, and even more difficult to live with when it arises. The supervisor has primary responsibility for sensitizing the therapist to hear and bear the brunt of the patient's feelings, fantasies, and distortions without withdrawing or retaliating. It takes a long time for a clinician to believe that the transference distortions of the patient are basically "addressed to occupant," and have little to do with the real qualities or defects of the therapist. Indeed, the patient may perceive the clinician as male or female, old or young, benevolent or evil—and all in relationship to the fantasied projections from the patient's emotional memory bank. In helping the clinician to become aware of these distortions, and in uncovering their accurate genetic origins with the patient, the supervisor teaches appropriate clinical distance, without which the clinician can hardly avoid feeling flattered, hurt, angered, or otherwise inappropriately responsive to the patient's expressions of feeling. The clinician will inevitably be drawn toward some of this excessive response in the patient by his own emotional history, and the two will resonate to some extent in the transference/countertransference phenomenon.

Typically, the therapist may overidentify with the patient and enter into a therapeutic misalliance, thereby colluding with the patient to avoid painful affects. Or, he may come to feel some repugnance for those patients whose expressions of neediness and passivity fly in the face of the helper's more active primary defenses. Thus the patient may feel discouraged from expressing these feelings by the clinician who is busy pointing out the patient's real competence when the patient is not feeling competent at all, but would also like to please the therapist from whom he needs all this help.

On the other hand, the therapist may take at face value the patient's criticism of the therapy and join in the patient's despair without understanding that this is a distortion due to the patient's transference.

It is left to the supervisor to point out these cases of psychological mistaken identity, and how they constitute an invaluable if confusing aspect of the material of the therapy. While they may lead to therapeutic and supervisory impasse (see Chap. 6), their recognition and management often signal a major advance in the clinician's movement toward professional maturity.

It is not enough to recognize the transference distortions; one must be able to decide what to do about them. In some therapeutic modalities they are noted but not addressed. In psychoanalytic psychotherapy, their interpretation is considered to be a primary curative factor. The supervisor helps to sort out the delicate questions of *timing*, of *appropriateness in terms of the working alliance with the patient*, of *accuracy*, and of the *tone* in which the transference will be brought to the patient's attention. A supervisor may offer examples of how he would intervene in such a situation, of what language he might use to question the accuracy of a patient's perceptions, etc. This kind of supervisory openness has obvious practical value, but also serves to remind the student that the supervisor is an ally in this difficult and often threatening endeavor.

In a trusting and open supervisory climate, the therapist can recognize the transference distortions, and his own response to them. While his countertransference is by definition unconscious, a respect for the familiarity with the transferential metaphor can relax some of the tension that is expectable in any clinician when he first learns to listen with the third ear to the patient's associations and gradually becomes aware of his own. As the therapist fears the distortions less, and indeed learns to value them, he comes to value his own as well, and to pay attention to them. The metaphor of the transference then becomes an arena in which both patient and therapist can join in the interplay that will release from repression unresolved conflicts and long-forgotten energy for growth and creativity.

Since transference is an ubiquitous phenomenon, manifestations of it will emerge between supervisor and therapist as well (6,7). As in the work with patients, the transference always provides a rich source of data. If a supervisor feels a student to be overly defensive in response to the gentlest critique, or too blindly compliant and eager to please, he can make tactful shifts in the work that will reduce the student's anxiety, address a similar problem in the patient—thus making use of the parallel process to resolve some of the student's transference problems toward him, or even raise the issue explicitly if the alliance will bear the confrontation. Similarly, if the supervisor becomes aware of an irrational counter-response to a student, he can be alerted to difficulties early enough to head off a potential impasse by seeking consultation, by self-examination, and by referring to the literature on techniques of supervision.

In sum, the supervisor must be as conscious of and tactful toward the transference dimension of the work with the trainee as he is teaching the student to be with the patient. The adjustment of the transference distortions in both cases stimulates health and creativity where there was once constraint and narrowness of vision.

E. Supporting the therapist

In a high-anxiety learning situation such as one finds in psychotherapy teaching, some of the primary needs of students are for support, hope, and optimism. Hope is a metastructure, an awareness and conviction of how things should be. It flourishes in change, uncertainty, and flux. It is distinguished from desire, which is implicated in the pleasure principle, and invested in the gratification of instincts (8).

In therapy, the clinician's desire to heal the patient and thus be gratified as a good and competent therapist may interrupt the patient's search for hope. The supervisor must help the clinician to tolerate the setting aside of short-term cures in favor of greater integration of the patient's own hopes and the gratification of the patient's own desires. The same discipline and hope also applies in the case of the supervisor/clinician dyad. Throughout this process of maturing hope, the supervisor models and lends ego to the student.

A supervisor supports by stimulating the student to see, to be curious, and to be creative, in the hope of achieving mastery overy the self and then becoming a competent, respected clinician—the professional definition of "how things should be." He provides an atmosphere of safety and optimism, in which the trainee can explore the frustrated hopes and dreams that he has encountered in the work with patients. He helps the student to grieve over the failure of some hopes, and works to avoid the student's clinical despair being directed toward the intractable patient, or toward therapy in general.

Supervisors are often confounded by the question of support, and wonder about how much support is appropriate. They tend to assume that the student is aware of their positive regard, or to minimize the importance of expressing it. Students are much clearer and unambivalent on the issue. They generally express a yearning for more positive regard from their supervisors. Without it, they feel anxiety and discouragement; this in turn interferes with their ability to accept the confrontation that is part of the work of effective supervision. Some of the earlier authors on the practice of supervision (9) even go so far as to state that the positive feelings of the supervisor or of the student are best left unaddressed lest they corrupt the learning.

It is interesting and a bit sad that students and supervisors both seem frequently to assume that one might be forced to forego high-powered intellectual learning and confrontation if a supervisor is supportive and reassuring. Whether this represents a Calvinistic assumption, or is a confusion of hope with desire, are open questions.

Support is often confused with inappropriate infantilization, and as such, has accumulated a bad press in the psychotherapy literature. In excess, it is certainly disabling and disarming, potentially interfering with aggression and learning. But on the other side of the question, too harsh and ascetic a stance may overstress the young clinician's object-hunger and loneliness. Outside of his own therapy hour, supervision is one of the few places where the clinician can talk about patients freely. Appropriate professional restraint is hard to bear, however, when one is excited and enthusiastic about the new work. The opportunity to safely discharge tension, express embarrassing fantasies, and share in a parental-like concern for the patient with the supervisor is at once stimulating and reassuring. It is a kind of professional communion that helps to avoid an inappropriate familiarity with the patient, or a tendency to carelessly chat about one's patients in more public settings, thereby risking a betrayal of the patient's trust and confidentiality. The supervisor can use these informal moments to reassure the therapist who may be anxious or ashamed of his feelings and fantasies toward the patients, to encourage a bit of bragging about therapeutic successes, and to otherwise exchange "war stories" that lend a human dimension to the work.

Another way of offering support is to participate in the acculturation of the young clinician. Most societies have subtle and powerful rites of passage for initiating newcomers into the inner circle, and the professional culture of the psychotherapist's world is no exception. The initiations confirm one's definition of the role and the self, and have been described as the greatest single factor ensuring mental development and stability (10). Confirmation is the stuff of which social reality is made. One of the major avenues to such confirmation in the professional culture of the psychotherapy world is the professional mentor. The main function of the mentor is to foster and confirm the therapist's aspirations, and to help the neophyte find practical ways to make them come true.

Supervisors mentor by contributing to the professional acculturation of the clinician in both political and practical ways. They have traditionally influenced the "nonspecific" aspects of a professional identity, such as habits of speech, even of dress. They provide access to new job opportunities, introduction to powerful figures in the field, both on social occasions and at professional conferences. They co-author journal articles. In addition, practical suggestions for establishing a private practice, referrals to such a practice, letters of recommendation, are all ways that supervisors help in the passage from student to professional.

Exclusion from this mentoring process has kept minority groups out of positions of power and influence in the field of psychotherapy as in every other field.

Women, for instance, suffer from the scarcity of other women in positions of power and prestige who might help initiate them

46

into the inner circles of the professional structure. Researchers (11–14) refer to the painful crippling isolation of minorities that inhibits growth and promotion. They see the necessity of belonging to a powerful legitimized community to lend confidence and practical access for professional attachment.

Finally, the supervisor offers another kind of support to both the student and to the training institution in the form of supervisory evaluations. This requires that he take very seriously the trust that is vested for quality control, and for future direction of all the parties concerned. In formal training programs, supervisors customarily provide a written evaluation of the student to the director of training once or twice a year. It is important that the supervisor share these evaluations with the trainee, negotiate with the student about their content, and use the evaluation process to support the clinician's future training by providing concrete guidelines for doing so.

Summary

In this chapter, supervision has been elaborated from the perspective of what supervisors do. This involves some concrete and some not so specific functions, all of which serve the development of the four parties to the clinical process. We have seen that part of what the supervisor does is to teach in a variety of ways. The dynamic nature of the supervisory dyad, however, is also based on the irrational involvement that the two have with each other. This temporary, subjective merger allows the young therapist to introject the best of the supervisor, and then to differentiate from that person to become an autonomous clinician.

Clearly, the relationship between the supervisor and the clinician is complex and involved; the involvement necessarily engages them both at levels of human interaction that are sometimes rational, sometimes not. This is a reality, but not necessarily a problem. "All psychological discovery," Freud wrote (15) "is accompanied by some irrational involvement of the observer, and cannot be communicated to another without a certain involvement of both." Because of the importance of the dyadic relationship to clinical development, it is crucial to understand the development of the supervisor over the course of his professional career. To do so requires an awareness of that particular supervisor's needs, hopes, life issues, and philosophy, and how these will impinge on what he does in the supervisory hour.

References

1. Alonso, A. & Rutan, J. Cross-sex supervision for cross-sex therapy. *Am. J. Psychiatry* 135(8): 928–931, 1978.
2. Blaxall, M. & Reagan, B. *Women and the Work-place.* Chicago: University of Chicago Press, 1976.
3. Boris, H. On hope: its nature in psychotherapy. *Int. J. Psychoanal.* 3:139–150, 1976.
4. Fleming, H. & Benedek, T. *Psychoanalytic Supervision.* New York: Grune & Stratton, 1966.
5. Freud, S. The dynamics of the transference (1912). In E. Jones (Ed.), *Collected Papers.* New York: Basic Books, 1959, Vol. II, p. 314.
6. Greben, S., Markson, E., & Sadavoy, J. Resident and supervisor: and examination of their relationship. *Can. Psychiatr. Assoc. J.* 18:475, 1973.
7. Greer, G. *The Female Eunuch.* New York: McGraw Hill, 1970.
8. Ibid.
9. Lower, R. Countertransference resistances in the supervisory situation. *Am. J. Psychiatry* 129(2): 156–169, 1972.
10. Millet, K., *Sexual Politics.* New York: Doubleday, 1970.
11. Reik, T. *Listening with the Third Ear.* New York: Grove Press, 2948.
12. Searles, H. F. Psychoanalytic Supervision in Collected Papers on Schizophrenia and related subjects. New York: p. 593, International Universities Press, 1965.
13. Seiden, A. Overview: research on the psychology of women. *Am. J. Psychiat.* 133:1111–1123, 1976.

14. Semrad, E. The organization of ego defenses and object loss. In D. M. Moriarty (Ed.) *The Loss of Loved Ones*, Springfield, Ill.: Charles C Thomas, 1967.

15. Waltzlawick, P. et al. *Pragmatics of Human Communication: A Study of Interactional Patterns, Pathologies and Paradoxes.* New York: Norton, 1967.

5

The Supervisor in Developmental Perspective

In tracing the development from youth to maturity, one recognizes issues salient to all adults at each stage of that passage. There is a time when making a commitment to intimacy supersedes the thrust for independence and differentiation.

Later there is a time for mentoring the young in their climb and for enriching and maintaining emotional and aesthetic ideals. Levinson speaks eloquently to the evolution of age-appropriate and related changes:

"Every season has its own time; it is important in its own right, and needs to be understood in its own terms. No season is better or more important than any other. Each has its necessary place and contributes its special character to the whole. It is an organic part of the total cycle, linking past and future, and containing both within itself"(1.).

In this chapter we will explore the normal developmental imperatives as they apply specifically in the work of supervisors of psychotherapy. Supervisors change over time. They supervise a certain way as they begin their careers, and move along a fairly predictable continuum throughout their professional lives. This development is influenced by a variety of factors surrounding the supervisory work. Some have to do with the supervisor's own definition of self in the role, some relate to the work with the students, and others to the context of the supervision. All are interwoven with the personal strands of the supervisor's life. As in a coarse weaving, a strong pull on any one strand can distort the whole, whereas a more finely integrated weaving offers greater resistance to damage from any one snag.

In addition to this linear development, supervisors are influenced by the dialectic forces from conservative to radical and back that synthesize in adult growth. Can the fervor and ideals of youth, the creative curiosity that tests new horizons and establishes new frontiers of human understanding combine in a healthy adaptation with the power and assurance that are the strength of maturity? Can they come to some integration in the psychotherapy supervisor in ways that provide a balance of creative experimentation and realistic wisdom? After all, the changes that occur in the course of a lifetime require a certain loss of innocence, even as they lead to the development of new resources and perspectives for the maturing individual. To what extent does the supervisor nourish the dream of his own early idealism, and his student's, and encourage whatever the student is capable of setting into creative flight, or on the other hand, how much of the accumulation of tempered conservative wisdom should the supervisor impose on the situation, lest the whole system or any of its parts suffer undue distress? Conversely, can the student catalize and rekindle the supervisor's curiosity and excitement so that both may experiment together, and learn from each other in a true mutuality?

These dilemmas are the fundamental "stuff" of supervision, and are related to the life continuum of the supervisor. Their resolution depends, in part, on the theoretical convictions of the supervisor and the constraints of the training situation, but each supervisor evolves idiosyncratic solutions by which he copes with the constraints. The imperatives of adult development merge with the personal life pressures, strengths, personality components, and prior failures and successes of the supervisor to influence the work with the therapist in the supervisory situation. Each supervisor sits at a certain point on this continuum, and each contributes significantly to the clinical development of the young therapist. The supervisor is, in turn, influenced by the relationship with the supervisee in a way that makes an impact on the supervisor's progression through his current life stage.

It is the integration of these forces, and their impact on the career span for supervisors that constitute the main thrust of this chapter. It consists of three major sections that span the supervisory career from novice, to mid-life, to late career. In each section, we will focus on three parameters of the supervisor's experience:

1. The development of a sense of self, and the maintenance of that identity as a supervisor.

2. The interpersonal relationship between the supervisor and the therapist-in-training.

3. The negotiation and maintenance of a healthy relationship with the training institution.

The novice supervisor

Typically, the new supervisor is close to thirty years old, and has completed a fairly rigorous course of academic training in the recent past. Thus, the beginning of a supervisory career probably will coincide with several major life events: (1) The launching of an autonomous professional career, either as a clinician in private practice or as an academic clinician; (2) The need to find, commit to, and/or maintain an intimate personal relationship; (3) The decision to have a child now, later, or ever. It is highly likely that he is torn in a conflict between these three. To find the time and leisure and peace of mind to cultivate a love life, a professional career, and start a family is no mean feat. There is general agreement in the adult development literature that these goals are pretty universal for people of middle-class western cultures, at this stage of life. Since supervisors of psychotherapy emerge predominantly from this population it is reasonable to assume the same applies to them.

For the new supervisor, the definition of self as a person who has completed a protracted training and is now an autonomous adult coincides with the beginning of a new career in which he usually has no training at all. To be sure, the career carries with it status and power at the same time that it threatens the recently established confidence in the clinical area.

On the positive side, the younger supervisor has affiliative needs that facilitate connectedness and identification with the trainee. He also remembers clearly what it is like to be supervised, and to experience the distress of the learning regression in training. However, he may feel confusion around the ill-defined supervisory role, and the conflict that comes with crossing role boundaries and joining one's mentors as a colleague. The simultaneous development can be more arduous for some than it is for others, and will affect that person's level of comfort or distress in the process of becoming a supervisor. It is not unusual for a novice supervisor to present a somewhat rigid stance with the trainee around the work, and feel threatened by the therapist's attempts at friendship; the supervisor may be feeling that he could work or play, be a supervisor or a friend, with little confidence about what constitutes a proper balance. These balancing skills are developed to some extent in the process of becoming a clinician, but there are some major differences in supervision. One's clinical training usually began a decade earlier, when the life tasks were quite different ones, such as separating from family of origin, resolving adolescent wars, and so forth. In addition, the work with patients is much more clearly defined, protected by the barriers of clinical distance and definitions of appropriate behaviors, and guided by careful supervision at the time. The new supervisor's quest for identity is a much less guided one. It is difficult for the new supervisor to bear being clumsy in the face of potential humiliation from colleagues and students alike. If asked, new supervisors often will admit that they feel fraudulent and are terrified of being discovered as such. What if the student asks an obvious question that the supervisor cannot begin to address? What if the trainee should drop out of supervision, or feel sorry for the novice supervisor? In short, will the supervisor prove to be lovable and worthy of respect, and will he be able to contribute effectively to the growth of the therapist? These goals of affiliation and competence are consistent with the developmental imperatives of the supervisor, and together will form the life "dream," professionally speaking.

Since there are few arenas for open discussion of a supervisor's insecurities, the novice must draw on related areas of experience. Typically, he will tend to recall the ego ideals who can be emulated in order to begin to establish a sense of self as a supervisor. Memories of former supervisors combine with memories of the experience of being supervised. For the first time the supervisor can see the process from both sides of the desk.

It is a rare and blessed clinician who can look back on the training experience with totally benevolent memories of supervision. Most had a range of supervisors, some of whom were inspiring, but a few of whom may have left the neophyte with some distress and a bruised self-esteem. The whole range of affective memories is awakened, and the young supervisor's initial identity emerges in the shadow of these "supervisory introjects." The emotional memories (introjects) of the admired supervisor are cherished for a lifetime.

> *EXAMPLE:* Dr. R. recalls with deep appreciation a supervisor in her first year of training who basically told her she was doing fine as often as he could, and regaled her with hilarious stories of his own flubs when he wanted to gently redirect her efforts. She had been extremely anxious, overly diligent and compliant, and his interventions calmed and reassured her in a way that left her open to learning from the more critical supervisors of her later training years. She spoke of this supervisor with misty-eyed devotion and loyalty, twenty years later.

The more difficult memories are no less important, and leave the neophyte supervisor with some negative guidelines; he can begin by saying, as do young parents, "At least I know not to do such and such with my trainee!" It is also true that as he begins to supervise, he begins to appreciate the complexity of the task and can forgive, or at least put into better perspective, the experience with the "offending" supervisor.

> *EXAMPLE:* Dr. W. has never forgotten the agony and embarrassment of an early supervisory experience. In his first year of training, he arrived at his first supervision with an eminent teacher, trembling but proud of having prepared for the hour by reading, annotating, and practically memorizing the hour with the patient. To his chagrin, after about five minutes the supervisor stopped him, chided him for not having the full data about the patient's early developmental history, proclaiming that the patient didn't sound like an appropriate therapy patient to him in the first place. This was so painful and humiliating for the young clinician that he vowed to never, never challenge a student in this offensive way when his turn came to supervise. He has, in fact, become a sought-after supervisor, and is very dedicated to and proud of this aspect of his career. Thus it was with some distress that he heard his student complain a bit that she felt over-scrutinized and over-controlled in the hour at times!

Because both positive and negative memories are so powerful, some aspects of that supervisor have been woven into the fabric of the learner's clinical identity and the supervisory ego-ideal. The ego-ideal, as defined by conflict theory is a merged "dream" that consists of a joining of one's best hopes for the self with the best view of the idealized other, whom one loves and wishes to emulate. It is the stuff of aspiration, and passion, and striving for excellence. But closely allied with the concept of ego-ideals is the concept of oedipal conflict and its ensuing anxiety.

Symbolically, Oedipal anxiety has come to refer to competition with parental or parental-like figures; this then would include supervisors and others in authority. The wish to succeed and in fact to supersede them stimulates ambivalence rooted in the unconscious oedipal complex of the adult, which persists throughout life (2). While the concept of oedipal anxiety is not addressed explicitly in the adult development literature, it is implicit in the tension that surrounds movement from one stage of development to another.

The move from trainee to supervisor is akin to the move of the son or daughter into the family business; it is a point of pride, but also of some anxiety and confusion. It involves the neophyte around both the concepts of ego-ideal and oedipal conflict. Freud defined the ego ideal as a transitional object that aids in the development of the individual from one level of maturity to the next. The individual moves away from the grandiose, narcissistic view of himself, transfers the idealization to an object (person) other than the self, and ultimately sublimates what is an essentially sexual instinct into the capacity to work. Aggressive instincts are also sublimated and joined to the libidinal ones, leading to creative mastery and excellence at work. In the case of the young supervisor, the work consists of the nurturance and care for the professional development of the supervisee.

However, the novice supervisor is somewhat at a loss when seeking ego-ideals, for although they exist in his/her own experience of being supervised, there has been little opportunity to learn explicitly about the process of supervision as it affects all parties concerned. The unconscious silence about the supervisors' part of the process and its effect on him mitigates against the student finding reassuring guidelines around which to organize the expectations arising from this new venture. This is in sharp contrast to the new supervisor's experience in learning to be a therapist, when many supervisors freely share their own memories and "tricks of the trade" with the student—an aspect which most trainees find comforting and enormously helpful.

Hamburg and Adams (3), in studying normal coping behaviors in the face of intense developmental stress, found that healthy people were able to cope by developing: (1) the capacity to seek and find information about the new situation in advance; (2) the ability to seek and find information about the new role requirements; (3) the ability to seek and acquire information about future difficulties; the utility of friendship in seeking new information.

In the early stage of supervising, the new supervisor is deprived of most of the coping options listed above, except in the technical sense. The information and advice available in the literature falls short of the full range of support possible and desirable for a budding career that will make huge demands on tact, knowledge, and interpersonal acuity. Thus the new supervisor is left to make decisions and to set directions by extrapolating from similar experiences from home, from clinical work, and from other related situations. As in all human choices, each leaves something to be desired, but also may offer new opportunities for creative thinking. The new supervisor can and does experiment with an integration of personal style, clinical philosophy, and theoretical conviction. He will emulate, more or less consciously, some of the better introjects from past experience and avoid some of the less helpful ones. Should personal conflicts be strongly stimulated by the role, or if the administration and/or the student prove to be overly disappointing or obstuctionistic, the novice is at risk of early disillusionment and despair about the fledgling supervisory career. But given that the novice is highly motivated for internal reasons as well as stimulated by the validation from teachers, former supervisors, and the appreciation of the supervisees, he has the opportunity to experience an emergent sense of self and self-confidence as a supervisor.

The novice supervisor and the therapist

The new supervisor and the trainee have much in common. From the perspective of adult development, they have similar life imperatives. For people in this third decade of life, (30 to 40, or therabout), there is a built-in conflict of directions for investing psychic energy. Both supervisor and student have to reconcile the personal needs for a stabilizing intimacy in their personal lives with the investment outside the self that is required for moving forth in a new career. For the supervisor, the need to establish equilibrium and mastery around affiliative wishes encourages his interest in the student, and in the partnership. Since they are roughly chronological equals, they are apt to share many of the same life issues, and thus present more accurate mirrors for one another. Neither can avoid being self-directed; both are struggling with the self-centered, narcissistic tasks that are normal and necessary. It is an age-appropriate time to be "selfish" about one's affiliative needs. Thus it can be difficult for the supervisor to put the therapist's needs first; on the other hand, to do so is to gratify vicariously some of his own similar wishes, so we are apt to find the novice supervisor closely identified with the student. He may focus almost exclusively on suggesting the use of better, more intelligent methods of treating the patient, who almost becomes a mutual patient. Insofar as this goal remains relatively free of transferential distortions, it is a fine idea, and certainly meets all the criteria of appropriateness. We might argue that the new supervisor is in an ideal position to offer concrete advice, since he is better able to remember how it feels to be on the receiving end of such advice.

The novice supervisor tends to be hampered by limited experience and confidence, however, and may become anxious should the therapist resist the advice that is offered. Usually, the younger supervisors are the more demanding and rigid about compliance; this is understandable given a limited supervisory repertoire and an eagerness and devotion to doing the job well. Nonetheless, he is prone to falling into a dilemma—expecting the supervisee to emulate the supervisor perfectly, which, if it were possible, would result in a mindless mimicry that parodies real learning. Thus, on the one hand, the new supervisor can empathize better with the student, but, on the other hand, he may need the student to comply in order to save them both from embarrassment. Another way of looking at this dialectic is to see the two poles as affiliation versus task orientation. The affiliative strengths are powerful between the two colleagues in this dyad, whereas the task orientation may be weaker or more brittle due to a shared lack of competence and inexperience.

As the new supervisor feels more secure in his capacity to survive in the role, i.e., to be a viable supervisory object for the trainee, he may become more vulnerable to strong competitive feelings toward the therapist who is, after all, a peer. Here they both must negotiate a Scylla-and-Charybdis problem. At best, the supervisor's competitive instincts can encourage a competitive climate that is safe, mutually exhilarating, and conducive to the two becoming increasingly powerful in their mutual roles. If the therapist proves clearly much less competent, however, the supervisor may feel threatened by the shadow of failure by identification with an incompetent near-peer.

> *EXAMPLE:* Dr. Jones made an appointment with the director of training, demanding to know why he had been assigned such an unsophisticated and naive student for the second year in a row. He was clearly very angry, and demanded to know the criteria for student selection, to participate in the decisions about acceptance in the future, and especially, not to be assigned to a "nincompoop" next year. In addition, he felt strongly that his first-year student be considered for discontinuance after only two months in the program. In discussion, it evolved that Dr. Jones had felt very badly about the marginal progress his student had made the year before, was anxious that the administration might be making some adverse judgments about the supervision, and that his efforts might not be valued in the future. In fact, he had done a fine piece of work with a very difficult situation, and the new student was assigned because the administration had been so impressed with his capacity to work well with a beginning student. When this was clarified, and the director of training had expressed thanks more forcefully for the supervisor's contribution, the supervision continued very successfully, to everyone's appreciation.

On occasion the supervisor may encounter a trainee who is brighter, taller, or especially skillful in an area where the supervisor feels clumsy. In the field of mental health, clinicians strive for a cooperative goal in which they can generously set aside their own agenda and work in the best interest of the more vulnerable party to the interaction. A clinician's self-esteem depends on his capacity to do so. When this generosity of spirit is threatened by competitive feelings, the supervisor is apt to judge himself harshly for wanting to "best" the student and come out looking superior.

In addition to controlling competitive feelings, the novice must also define appropriate levels of intimacy with the trainee. Since intimacy is an overriding concern of both, much energy is available in each for closeness. The supervisory situation sets the stage for closeness, both by its regularly scheduled contact, and by the very private and often intense patient material that is discussed, which stimulates the emotions of all parties to the interaction. Both essentially become pseudoparents to the patient being presented; in this pairing, fantasies of sexual intimacy may emerge, leading to feelings of guilt and secrecy. If these fantasies are acted out in any of a variety of ways, they ultimately can threaten the supervision and the therapist's clinical development. Held in perspective, they allow for the emergence of a tenderness and concern for the patient, and an affectionate working relationship between supervisor and trainee. The new supervisor's awareness of such affects remains the best safeguard against regressive acting-out of instinctual drives, consistent with the basic tenets of psychodynamic therapy.

Searles states that "competitiveness in the more usual sense of the word, in the supervisory relationship has at times appeared to me as a defense against the students' and my being drawn together in compassion"(4).

In sum, the novice supervisor is seen to resemble an older sibling—one who still remembers what it feels like to be in the therapist's place, but for whom the competitive issues are still hot. The mutual availability for intimacy and affiliation potentially holds them together in an alliance that provides for the maturation of both parties.

The novice supervisor and the administrative establishment

As the supervisor struggles to become an appropriate overseer of the therapist's development, a conflict arises sooner or later over divided loyalties between therapist and administration. To the novice supervisor still gaining confidence, the threat of a split between the parties is a particular threat because one or the other, it is feared, will then call into question the competence that the supervisor is working to establish.

The supervisor is still close to his own memories of feeling intimidated and abused by the administration when he was a trainee, and may still harbor some angry feelings that resonate with the supervisee's. The supervisor has, however, at this point, some of the wisdom of hindsight, and this perspective may help neutralize and channel some of their shared residual anger and defiance toward the training institution and toward authority in general.

The transformation of anger into strength was described by Freud as "the multifariously perverse sexual disposition of childhood," which when converted and sublimated becomes the source of creative new ideas. Vaillant (5), too, delineates the more mature defenses that lead to instinctual sublimation and healthy adaptation. He lists: (1) suppression, (2) anticipation, (3) altruism, and (4) humor. All four are available in the new supervisor, and supported by the demands of the role. In the "with a grain of salt" perspective that new graduates are apt to hold toward the dicta and constraints of the institution, there is ample capacity for the supervisor to apply support and even humor to the young therapist's struggles and bruises. In cases of insolvable difficulties, the therapist may turn to the supervisor for ways around the dilemma with more confidence than he might to a more senior supervisor who is more entrenched in the administration.

In addition to the ombudsman role, the novice supervisor offers the administration an infusion of energy and optimism toward negotiating a balance of investment in student training, patient care, and other workings of the department, such as research or liaison with other systems. The new supervisor's ambitions are clearly on the side of training, and he plainly represents that position to the administration with the freshness and eagerness that comes with the ambition of youth. If the more entrenched members of the administration are able to accept and welcome the new supervisor's contribution, this sense of acceptance and openness will be transmitted down to the therapist-in-training as well. By this I mean that a respectful and eager attitude toward inexperienced newcomers stimulates excitement and creativity in the whole system. If Szasz (6) is correct in assuming that august institutions become inhibitors of the creative process, then the novice supervisor has some advantage because he has not been subject to this ossification, and can serve to champion the supervisee's imaginative thinking.

Another developmental need of the young supervisor is to find a place in the community in which he can render civic service and lay down roots. His contribution to the training system is a channel for these needs, and an important aspect of maturity and adulthood. The statement is made to the world at large that the individual has accepted citizenship in a professional community of highly valued individuals who make a major contribution to the world in which they work and live. He becomes that institution's representative in the general community and shapes and influences the future of the profession. He may look forward to assuming leadership in that department and thereby communicate a hopefulness that transmits to the institution and to the students as well.

The supervisor at mid-career

By the time an individual has reached mid-life, many of the young person's questions about the definition of self have been answered. The earlier conflict and turmoil that accompany the emergence of a stable sense of self have mellowed. Issues of professional ambitions have become clearer. The individual begins to arrive at a more realistic sense of whether one should aspire to a Nobel prize, or settle for the more ordinary course of a career. The acceptance of compromise has reduced some distress around the limits of human endeavor, and with this acceptance the individual finds more psychic energy to devote to the care and mentoring of the people in his surround. The self-preoccupation about one's sense of wholeness and stability gives way to an increasing interest in the people and world outside the self, and outside of one's most intimate circle of family and friends.

The net effect of this integration of the self at mid-life is an expansion of generosity and empathy. Erik Erikson (1978) describes this movement from concern for the self to concern for others, as follows: "The passions of the temperament and the loyalty of the heart, or the potency of the genitals and the generosity of the womb, which serve erotic and procreative union, are sumblimated for higher endeavors, or left below and to be avoided"(7).

More recently, Kernberg (1980) relates the development of healthy narcissism to the healthy development of the self, and pathological narcissism to a disorder in the self definition. Of particular relevance here are the seven life tasks that he assigns to middle age. They include:

1. Shift in time perspective. The past and the present begin to merge more strongly than was previously possible due to an increased understanding. . . . "the activation of reciprocal roles stemming from internalized object relations of the past brings about an increasing awareness of and coming to terms with identifications reflecting the entire life span"(8).

2. Reversal in external and internal rates of change. The outside world appears to be in greater flux during middle age. This increases the mourning processes associated with loss and separation.

3. The limits of creativity. One has to learn to accept the limitations of one's ability to accomplish. This diminishes jealousy, shame, and envy.

4. Ego identity in the perspective of time. "The task of middle age is to reconcile one's knowledge of one's future derived

from knowledge about one's past, with the acceptance of risk"(9). There is also the necessity of acceptance of the inherent conflicts in intimate relationships and the containment of them in a stable relationship. Kernberg indicates that this may indeed be the major task of middle life.

5. Coming to terms with external aggression. One must accept that there is indeed badness in the world in which one lives. One must live by one's own ego ideals and accept the fact that the final responsibility is to oneself.

6. Loss, mourning, and death. "The sense of accepting what one has accomplished, with all its limitations, helps in accepting death as a final statement of 'mission accomplished'"(10).

7. Oedipal conflicts. The Oedipus complex, according to Kernberg, takes on a new perspective during this period of time due to the intergenerational patterns and relationships. One is faced with diminishing envy toward the separating and individuating child whose future is filled with potential and possibility, at the same time that one is faced with coming to terms with the death of one's own parents and the accompanying guilt and loss. The resolution parallels the incorporation of the superego except in this case, "the reinstatement of the parents as object representations, and of their world as an internal object world reflects the love toward them and persistent object investment in them and in what they stand for"(11).

To put these concepts into the context of the mid-life supervisory career, specific milestones have been reached, such as the completion of one's own treatment or analysis; a clinical focus has been concentrated, decisions have been made about research or writing as a viable aspect of the professional career. The most common altruistic aspect of the career of mid-life clinicians is the dedication to the supervision and training of younger clinicians. Once again the supervisor's developmental tasks and supervisory work are complementary to one another.

Levinson describes three mid-life polarities pertinent to supervisors at mid-career: (1) The Young/Old polarity, (2) The Destruction/Creation polarity, (3) The Male/Female polarity.

1. THE YOUNG/OLD POLARITY

Awareness of the finiteness of time and of one's own mortality generates in the individual at mid-life a need to take stock of what really has meaning for him/her. If the process of narrowing down is to be purposeful and select, then one must focus in on some areas and relinquish others. To fail to do so leaves the individual vulnerable to a sense of defeat or spread thin in a set of shallow life investments.

Stock taking is to some extent intrinsic to the work of supervision. One must be prepared to explain, defend, and inspire the student to invest in a shared set of theoretical assumptions. In the process, the supervisor must take a hard look at his/her own theoretical base, must be prepared to defend without being doctrinaire or rigid, to deepen the dialogue around the work, and to acknowledge the limits of his/her own position. This consciousness of professional self comes easier for the mid-career supervisor than for the neophyte for whom the age-appropriate position is still one of search and trial. There is an emphasis upon introspection and stocktaking, upon conscious reappraisal of the self. There is conscious self-utilization rather than the self-consciousness of youth"(12).

2. THE DESTRUCTION/CREATION POLARITY

The acute sense of one's own ultimate destruction awakens in people at mid-life an urge to create, as well as to redress grievances with people whom one may have damaged in the past. There is a need to convey meaning about the present, to forgive the past, and to plan for as generative a future as one can hope for. The opportunity to exercise altruism toward the trainee and toward the clinical field is in harmony with the internal imperatives. In the work with the student, the supervisor is called upon to communicate meanings that dignify the professional investment. When the student asks, "Why am I doing this difficult work?", the supervisor is pressed to articulate once again those aspects of the profession that have maintained their meaning, and rediscovers them in concert with the supervisee. For the mid-career supervisor, the old feelings of therapeutic despair are diminished, and in their place he finds a feeling of excitement and fruition, blended with some resignation around the more confining limits of the clinical possibilities.

At this stage also, as one comes to accept the disappointments of the past, one finds that there was much of value that had remained unappreciated in the less forgiving mood of the earlier years. Mark Twain once commented that his father had gained remarkable intelligence in the three years since he had seen him last. So it is with the old teachers from the supervisor's past, who can now be appreciated and their wisdom re-integrated anew into one's own teaching.

3. THE MALE/FEMALE POLARITY

In the early twentieth century, the assumptions in the literature about traditional roles for the sexes led to naturally rigid assumptions of normal male and female roles. More recently, with the evolution of psychological thinking and a more sophisticated view of differences between men and women, we can translate more appropriately the notions of anima/animus (Jung) to include a reintegration of all the previously disowned male or female aspects of the self. One of the major debates in the theories of adult development and of gender development relates to the dual aspects of affiliation and work. While male theorists have tended to see these two areas as developing cyclically and separately, female writers have described development as simultaneous, at least for women, and perhaps for all people. The latter (13,14) believe that development is continuous and simultaneous, with some balance between affiliation and aggression (or work); a major imbalance is seen a pathological if it persists over a period of time. Freud too is said to have measured the "good life" in terms of the capacity to love and to work. The experience of what constitutes a successful balance of affiliation and work, however, seems to differ in men and women. Gilligan writes that women experience maturity and success in terms of an increasing responsibility for the care and well-being of others, while for men, maturity and success is seen as an opportunity to exercise the prerogatives of right and power. At mid-life, this polarity decreases, with both men and women acknowledging a blend of the two, rather than a choice of one over the other.

In the supervisory career, affiliation and aggression, or love and work, find a natural blending and integration without which clinical learning will not occur. Similarly, the male and female aspects of the supervisor are called upon if he is to empathize with the student of either gender, causing the supervisor to explore and rediscover the disowned aspects of the self once again. Both grow together into more complete human beings, and the supervisor's generative instincts are well served in the process.

The mid-career supervisor and the therapist

An individual's capacity to relate to another follows from the clarity and stability of his sense of self. The relationship with the therapist whom one supervises is reflective of the supervisor's sense of professional identity, and the pride one takes in that identity. By now, the supervisor has ideally modulated the perfectionism and criticalness characteristic of supervisors in their earlier years. With a well established sense of professional self, the supervisor can now turn toward helping and investing in the therapist as never before; this shift provides the climate in which the therapist can look for and find mentoring from the supervisor. The relationship develops along the parameters of nurturance, competition, and intimacy.

1. Nurturance

The mid-career supervisor is an ideal mentor. Half a generation older than the therapist, midway between peer and parent, he is in a position to look both ways. He possesses enough expertise and authority to help pave the way, understands that there are many roads to Rome, and also that time is finite, and one cannot "prepare" forever. This allows for a more accepting attitude toward the student's limitations and strengths.

Similarly, the supervisor is in a better position to be philosophical about boundaries and limitations, and to be more optimistic about the student's capacity to grow through impasses similar to those he had to overcome. Because of this optimism, the supervisor can *better* let go of some of the fantasies and needs to control the supervisee's activities more readily, and, from a true mentoring position, simply guide, encourage, and stimulate the supervisee in his own development.

2. Competition

Although the supervisor has made peace with major life decisions, there remains for everyone remnants of the more grandiose dreams that were put aside for the compromise. These are restimulated and rise to the surface again as the young therapist presents a vision of boundless options and the enthusiasm of an "everything-is-possible" stance vis-á-vis the world, including the clinical work. Thus if the supervisor, having decided to concentrate on being a clinician and a supervisor, hears his supervisee expound on the excitement of a career in research, or a fellowship that provides two years in the exotic tropics for studying the influence of leisure on the obsessive personality, the supervisor may experience more than a little envy and outrage.

But envy has two sides. It consists of hatred toward someone who has something the individual desires, and admiration of him for just that reason.

Envy can be felt by both the supervisor and the therapist. If the supervisor has to struggle with the feelings outlined above, the therapist also feels envious of the supervisor's power, status, and relative professional autonomy.

In mid-career, the supervisor is at his professional prime. It has become fairly clear by now whether one's career is going to be brilliant, average, or modest. It is possible to compare one's own level of success and compromise with that of influential figures from the past. If the supervisor measures up to personal and generational expectations, then he is in a better position to approve of and to support the increasing coming-of-age of the supervisee with some relish, since the latter will be seen as carrying on the legacy. If, on the other hand, the supervisor falls far short of earlier personal aspirations, then the bright and ambitious supervisee is apt to stimulate feelings of shame and anger in the supervisor, who may then view the student as a young upstart.

3. Intimacy

At mid-career, the supervisor's personal life tasks include an investment of energy in the issues of separation and individuation. The children are getting older and leaving home, parents are dying, and some of the dream has been tempered by harsh reality. This presents the supervisor with a double-edged sword.

On the one side, the supervisee is the perfect "replacement object," the promise of children forever, and for that matter, of parents forever, insofar as the supervisor is vicariously gratified in parenting the student. The latter, however, must begin to differentiate from the mentor and ultimately to reject this previously beloved figure, at least temporarily—thus creating a developmental crisis for both. Like all developmental crises it offers the potential for future growth and wisdom, but the process causes pain for all concerned.

Supervisors, when discussing this issue, respond with affect-laden memories, some of which graphically illustrate the conflict: One supervisor describes traveling many miles to give a paper at the request of a former student—only to find that the student himself had not planned to attend. Another speaks of her dismay at hearing a recent student confide to her that one of his patients has made notable progress since he had begun using new treatment methods under the tutelage of Dr. X. A third supervisor describes feelings of ambivalent pride and envy at seeing his recent student's fourth publication appear in less than one year.

Supervisees often report angry final supervisory reports that come like bolts from the blue, leaving students reeling with shock and feelings of painful betrayal at the hands of a formerly trusted supervisor. The intensity of these affects (15) usually results in a final and wrenching good-bye; possibly this represents an unconscious acting-out of the issues of grief and loss in the supervisor—an attempt to master feelings about the impending loss of the student and the dream he symbolizes, along with other feelings that the supervisor has no legitimate place to express. Supervision can and should allow for the sublimation of these anxieties about loss and grief, and provide an opportunity to the supervisor for expressing generativity: ". . . . every mature adult knows the satisfaction of explaining what is dear to him and of being understood by a groping mind. Care is the widening concern for what has been generated by love, necessity, or accident; it overcomes the ambivalence adhering the irreversible obligation" (16).

The mid-career supervisor and the administration

Having experienced the administrative mechanism for several years, the mid-career supervisor can add to his mentoring capacity an in-depth knowledge of the ins and outs of the institution and help the students negotiate the political waters more adeptly than they might on their own. The fact that the supervisor has chosen to remain with the institution indicates that he is convinced that the goals and integrity of the institution are worthwhile. Because the supervisor may also serve in other roles such as an administrative or training committee member, he will be in a position to clarify confusion surrounding those institutional areas, and to report back to the institution suggestions offered by the supervisee. This two-way function can reduce the therapist's feeling of helplessness in the face of the administration's present policies.

The task of reporting back is freer and more objective at this stage. The supervisor is secure in his position in the department, and is able to trust the manner in which the administration will react to his communication about a given student. He is far less vulnerable to the we/they split and the conflict about authority that is innate in novice supervisors. Aware of his value to the institution he is less apt to take any lack of progress by the student/therapist personally, and is in a better position to examine his own contribution to the supervision, both for good and ill.

In sum, the mid-career supervisor is in prime condition for the optimal fulfillment of the job. Secure in career choice and personal competence as both a clinician and a supervisor, somewhat settled in personal life choices and position, he seeks to develop the generative aspects of the self professionally and finds opportunity to do so via the work with the supervisee. The therapist/trainee offers a vehicle for a new Young/Old integration as described in Levinson and others:

"The task in every transition is to create a new Young/Old integration appropriate to that time of life. Especially with the change in eras, there is normally an increase in the old qualities of maturity, judgment, self-awareness, magnanimity, integrated structure, breadth of perspective. But these qualities are of value only if they continue to be vitalized by the Young's energy, imagination, wonderment, capacity for foolishness and fancy. The Young/Old connection must be maintained." (17).

The supervisor at late career

The major contribution made by the adult developmentalists is their insistence that an individual's identity is never beyond change, and that indeed, the capacity to change throughout the entire life span is a major determinant of mental health. Neugarten sums up the adaptations of older people: " . . . this ability to interpret the past and to foresee the future, to create for oneself a sense of the predictable life cycle, presumably differentiates the healthy adult personality from the unhealthy" (18). Erikson spoke of his own experience in immigrating as an adult, and needing to redefine a sense of self without familiar landscape and language, and missing the references on which his first sensory and sensual impressions were based. Age can impel a redefining of the terrain, because the person who has not adequately solved his identity problem earlier finds his life is not quite acceptable to him as the only life he will ever have. The avenue for the development of a rich identity in the later years is the capacity to be generative, and to invest in sharing wisdom with the young.

Any fulfillment of the individual at the end of the life cycle depends on moving far beyond the goals of terminal clarity about the self and the world around; one must remain responsible for contributing to the continuity of the generations and to the world in a personally satisfying way. Fidelity to the earlier meaningful structures is an alternative to a state of self-absorption and despair.

Supervision is an ideal medium for the exercise of the developmental prerogatives at the later end of the life cycle. The supervisor's sense of self is integrally attached to the generativity afforded him by the fulfillment of the trainee's needs.

The supervisor faces in his personal life a diminishing circle of peers; parents are gone, and so to some extent so are physical strength and beauty. One faces the prospect of personal loneliness. The motivation is great to take stock, and to find new people to validate, and be validated by in return. One's self is besieged from many directions, and one is dependent more than ever on prior resources and adjustments. In addition to personal shifts, he may experience pressure to make professional shifts, may be accused of being outdated and doctrinaire, and not in tune with the newest developments in the field. How the supervisor manages these tensions will determine the course of the rest of his professional career. The choice is between hope, wisdom, and integrity, and clinical despair and boredom. In the work of supervision, he encounters the opportunity to integrate old skills with new, to enlarge his repertoire rather than to constrict it, to refresh the mind and rejuvenate the soul.

The late career supervisor and the therapist

The older supervisor has at hand a lifetime of wisdom born of perspective and experience. He has trained many students, and by now will probably experience very few surprises of a disturbing nature. There is a familiarity of logic, and predictability of therapeutic dilemmas that can be applied to understand most supervisory presentations. A critical advantage is the supervisor's ability to predict the flow of the treatment with some accuracy and perspective. The long view, or literal "overseeing" of a situation is the essence of the late-career supervisor's advantage.

For the student, the opportunity to learn from a senior supervisor offers a cross-generational perspective that can provide empathy, wisdom, and understanding for patients much older than oneself, as well as increased respect for the competence of old age. Free from the need to compete with the student, the supervisor can exercise all the pleasures and prerogatives of a benevolent grandparent. He can now take in stride the stressful situations involving frightening patients, other supervisors, and the administrative vicissitudes around which he has seen the pendulum swing once or twice in the past. In addition, the supervisor has a wealth of hope and experience from which he can draw to teach, encourage, and comfort the clinician.

Having accumulated quite a few clinical successes, and survived a few failures, the older supervisor may not need the student to be quite so successful, and so is able to respond less defensively to the supervisee's challenges to "gospel truths" often propounded by the earlier supervisors, many of whom may be at the peak of theorizing and speech-making careers. The supervisee, relieved of the oedipal anxiety of dealing with the supervisors who are near-parents, may be able to learn and experiment more creatively.

On the other hand, the supervisor may have to bear from the supervisee some of the unconscious scorn the young can have for the old in this culture. To the extent that the supervisor can notice and tactfully take up this issue in supervision, to that extent he has helped the therapist correct what would have constituted a serious limitation to the work with older patients and colleagues.

The supervisor who has resolved the conflict between generativity and despair in the direction of generativity will have negotiated another level of growth while enhancing the development of the young professional in the system. Maturity of this kind characterizes, at its root, the highest quality of life.

The late career supervisor and the administration

Supervisors can exert maximal power and influence with the administration at this stage of life. They have usually accomplished their personal goals, and can work more selflessly for the department. To the extent that this is true, these years may be the least conflicted in terms of their relationship with the administration of the training institution. Seen as no threat to the power structure, valued for their long experience and wisdom by the hierarchy, with leisure time enough to serve on committees, they represent a rich resource for the institution, and the institution, in turn, offers them a chance to continue what they most love to do.

Still, the aging supervisor is at the mercy of the good offices of the institution if he wishes to continue to earn a living in part by supervising young trainees. In a shrinking economic climate for mental health care, many supervisors have found themselves pressured to teach courses, administer programs, or treat patients in the hours previously set aside for supervision. They may be asked to supervise for no financial remuneration. It is at this juncture that the struggle between generativity and rejectivity reaches its nadir. Whether to withdraw and write or keep the commitment to supervision presents a serious conflict. Training institutions have not prepared themselves to deal with this life event; more senior supervisors are being lost as a resource, and the pressure is on clinicians one or two years out of training to do the bulk of the supervision, resulting in a general constriction of the learning process for all involved.

Researchers in the area of late adult development (19–21) indicate that the mature individual measures the self in terms of biological health, psychological health, and his level of social awareness and contribution. In contributing to the development of the larger training institution, the older supervisor finds avenues for generativity and integration.

Ultimately, the supervisor at late career finds that he is looking to the student/therapist for successors to carry on the torch, and the memory of his role into posterity. If he feels fulfilled and proud of the legacy he can share it unambivalently and is in a position to be generous with wisdom and hope and praise for the future of the field and those who labor in it.

"Wisdom", says Erikson (1978), "is the detached and yet active concern with life itself in the face of death itself, and . . . maintains and conveys the integrity of experience in spite of the disdain over human failings and the dread of ultimate nonbeing" (22).

References

1. Levinson, D. J. *The Seasons of a Man's Life*. New York: Alfred A. Knopf, Inc., 1978, p. 7.
2. Brenner, C. *The Mind In Conflict*. New York: International Univ. Press, Inc., 1982, pp. 121–123.
3. Hamburg, D. A., & Adams, J. E. A perspective on coping behavior. *Am. General Psychiatry* 17: 277–284, 1967.
4. Searles, H. *Collected Papers on Schizophrenia and Related Subjects*. New York: International Univ. Press, 1965, p. 601.
5. Vaillant, G. E. *Adaptation to Life*. Boston: Little Brown & Co., 1977, p. 105–126.
6. Szasz, T. Psychoanalytic training: A socio-psychological analysis of its history and present status. *Int. J. Psychoanal.*, 39:598–613, 1958.
7. Erikson, E. *Adulthood*. New York: W. W. Norton Co., Inc., 1978, p. 21.
8. Kernberg, O. *Borderline Conditions and Pathological Narcissism*. New York: Jason Aronson, Inc., 1975, p. 125.
9. *Ibid.*, p. 128.

10. *Ibid.*, p. 129.

11. *Ibid.*, p. 134.

12. Neugarten, B. Dynamics of transition of middle age to old age: adaptation and the life cycle. *J. of Geriatric Psychiatry,* 4: 71–87, 1978.

13. Gilligan, C. *In A Different Voice.* Cambridge: Harvard U. Press, 1982.

14. Loevinger, R. & Wessler, R. *Measuring Ego Development.* San Francisco: Jossey-Bass, 1970.

15. Searles, *Op. Cit.*, p. 603.

16. Erikkson, E. *Insight and Responsibility.* New York: W. W. Norton Co., Inc., 1964, p. 131.

17. Levinson, D. J. *The Seasons of a Man's Life.* New York: Alfred A. Knopf, Inc., 1978, p. 212.

18. Neugarten, *Op. Cit.*, p. 79.

19. Birren, J. *The Psychology of Aging.* Englewood Cliffs, NJ: Prentice Hall, 1964.

20. Glenn, N. D. Psychological well-being in the post-parental stage: some evidence from national surveys. *J. Marriage and the Family.* February: 105–110, 1975.

21. Gould, R. *Growth and Change in Adult Life.* New York: Simon & Schuster, 1978.

22. Erikson, E. *Adulthood.* New York: W. W. Norton Co., Inc., 1978, p. 26.

6

The Supervisor
at Impasse

Given the complexity of the relationships in the supervisory situation, it is no surprise that the parties to the supervision will occasionally find themselves checkmated in their work. The supervisor is expected to be a teacher, a mentor, an administrator, a role model, a disciplinarian, and parental-like in his/her regard for the supervisee. These many roles often produce paradoxical effects, and can exert great pressure on the supervisor as well as on the therapist. As in all hierarchical situations, the temptation is to blame the person further down the ladder when things go wrong. The problem with this solution, apart from its obvious inequity, is that this leaves the supervisor with little sense of what can be done to improve the situation.

This chapter is devoted to the exploration of supervisory impasse—its causes, its many forms, and its consequences. Some examples are offered of impasse and its resolution. It is far beyond the scope of this work to make definitive suggestions that can claim to be universally effective for the resolution of impasse; the research is yet to be done that will enable us to offer scientific guidelines for impasse resolution. Yet, there are some commonly occurring and observable phenomena that merit careful study and exploration. The examples herein are offered to stimulate the reader's imagination and memory, and to share some observations about an extremely difficult problem that is an integral part of the supervisory function and career. Thus we will explore some of the probable causes of supervisory impasse, study some examples of difficulties in the work, and attempt to demystify the process so that the parties can disentangle from the confusion and allow for the supervision to proceed. In particular, we will focus on the supervisor's contribution to the impasse, with the understanding that this is hardly the only source of difficulty.

Students have trouble using supervision in a variety of ways. They most often have difficulty using supervision well because of dumb spots (1), or the simple lack of information on the student's part, which is easily remedied by teaching facts of theory or of technique. Blind spots arise from areas of mutual conflict between patient and therapist that make it difficult for the therapist to accept a supervisor's efforts to explore aspects of the patient that the therapist is avoiding in himself. Some patients develop a very intense transference toward the clinician, with demands that are hard to bear. An example of this is the feeling of dread that a student may experience in thinking about and reporting an hour with a severely devaluing patient who makes the student feel bad or repelled by the patient. While the more experienced clinician will recognize his response as normal, and a source of important data about the patient, the beginner is much more apt to be harshly judgmental of such responses in himself, and to assume that the supervisor will also cast blame. Areas of chronic unresolved conflict in the student generate true countertransference reactions that will perennially interfere with learning to be a psychotherapist, until they are resolved in the student's personal therapy. Another student may have personal difficulties with learning that have to do with a personality style. For example, a very well organized, obsessive-compulsive student may feel too much anxiety to tolerate the amorphous affect that is inherent in the learning of psychotherapy. Unmanageable personality differences that disable the competence of both people in the supervisory dyad also occur from time to time.

Other sources of difficulty stemming from the student are an inherent lack of faith in the psychotherapeutic process, or great doubts about the validity of the theories that the supervisor is espousing. The student may have unusual difficulty with empathy and alliance formation due to personal limitation, cultural bias, or naiveté.

> *EXAMPLE:* Dr. S. had begun his residency after some prior training in a highly biologic program, in which he was taught that only biological interventions made any sense in the treatment of psychosis. He chose an analyst as his supervisor in order to learn a new theory and technique, but he could not overcome his bias; he scorned the supervisor's input, and resisted any attempts to discuss the differences as a way of bridging the theoretical positions. The supervision ended badly, with both parties feeling anger and despair about their ability to be effective with the other party.

The administration may be contributing to supervisory impasse by undercutting the supervision, either directly or subtly. For example, a community mental health clinic made no pretense of valuing supervision except as a luxury to be indulged in if there were no patients waiting to be seen. They refused to allow supervision to be conducted in any of the clinical offices unless the supervisory dyad agreed to be interrupted at any time that the office was needed, by anyone needing to do clinical work with patients. Often supervision would be conducted in the clinic kitchen, or on the stairwell, with both parties feeling a little illicit for engaging in an activity that is perceived as frivolous.

At other times, too many people may get involved in the management of a patient, thus interfering with the work of the supervisor/therapist dyad.

EXAMPLE: Ms. V. is the daughter of a prominent physician in town; when she appeared at the clinic for psychotherapy, she was seen by a rather defensive, albeit competent resident, and for a while the work proceeded well. Soon, however, her pathology began to emerge, including some suicidal talk that frightened her and her therapist. In supervision, the resident presented a sublimely confident stance, refusing to acknowledge that the special status of the patient might be causing some anxiety over and above the normal anxiety that anyone might experience in a similar situation. The patient's father then called the department chief, who in turn called the supervisor to "check" on the situation. The supervisor felt the pressure to take over the case by insisting on telling the resident what to do, and abandoning the supervisory stance for one of control and criticism. Chaos ensued until the patient was transferred to a private clinician, and it was some time before the parties in the supervisory relationship could re-establish trust and enough respect to proceed. To their credit, this dyad managed to do so, and the impasse was resolved.

These are just a few examples of supervisory difficulty that have their origins outside the supervisor. With this in mind, let us turn to the supervisor, and try to understand the difficulties that may lead him to bring the work to a stalemate.

General considerations

Supervision is a difficult word to hear clearly. It stimulates emotional responses laden with superego affects. The word implies superior status, and a measure of control exercised over another. Fantasies and realities of power coexist alongside the supervisor's need to be loved, admired, trusted, and remembered fondly. They may interfere with the supervisor's realistic responsibility to exercise authority and to provide appropriate limits.

Another source of potential conflict is generated by the supervisor's dual loyalties to both student and to administration. The supervisor must negotiate a sometimes awkward middle course beween administration and supervisee, offering confidentiality and support for creative risk-taking to the student, and quality and safety standard setting to the administration.

For example, a supervisor may feel that he is working with a too-docile student who may not be learning in any depth because of the student's tendency to negotiate a very conservative and safe course—one that is beyond reproach. He may refer a difficult patient to a more senior clinician prematurely, or may employ several therapeutic modalities at once to cover all bases. There are arguments to be made for these approaches if they are decided upon thoughtfully, but the new clinician may be ill served if the choices lead him to avoid the anxiety of sorting out, thinking through, and learning to trust his own instincts. On the other side of the dilemma is the administration's need to avoid trouble in the form of repeated missed appointments by a difficult patient, or vulnerability to litigation, or cost effectiveness as defined and mandated by review boards. A similarly knotty problem surrounds the assignment of cases to a particular supervisee; the supervisor must make a balanced choice between service to whatever patients need treatment on the one hand, versus the need to vary the clinician's case load for optimal learning.

These decisions take on a Solomon-like cast; when combined with developmental stresses and changes in the personal and professional life of the supervisor, the process of supervision can get confusing and difficult. Sometimes these difficulties reach impasse proportions. Impasse here is defined as a stalemated conflict between supervisor and therapist or administration that resists resolution by logic or standard supervisory technique.

The supervisor's contribution to impasse

Supervisors contribute to conflict in the supervisory relationship. The etiology of these difficulties is complex and has many aspects that are idiosyncratic for each supervisor. Still, there are some common sources of difficulty that can restrict the effectiveness of a supervisor. These are; (1) The need to be admired, (2) the need to rescue, (3) the need to be in control, (4) the need to compete, (5) the need to be loved, (6) the need to work through unresolved prior conflicts in the supervisor's own training experience, and (7) spillover from stress in the personal or professional life of the supervisor that is overwhelming, and that contaminates all of his work, including the work of supervision.

The following section will examine each of these categories in some detail, and give some illustrations drawn from the experience of supervisors from a number of disciplines, at differing levels of seniority and expertise.

1. THE NEED TO BE ADMIRED

One of the factors which might lead people to a strong interest in psychology and psychiatry is an unconscious, sublimated identification with God (2). Charismatic leaders have a tendency to fall prey to fantasies of grandiosity that blind them to the reality of their situations, and the people with whom they interact (3–5). Supervisors of psychotherapy have the mantle of benevolent superiority, even in their titles. One of the major problems is that authority figures begin to believe in their own godliness, setting the stage for expectations that they will be adored and obeyed.

> *EXAMPLE:* Dr. G. is a powerful, charismatic figure who lectures and writes prolifically in a subspecialty of the clinical field. His work is familiar to many clinicians, and he is infamous for his arrogant but nonetheless effective style. He insists that his trainees write and perform publicly in exactly the style that he espouses, and is extremely intolerant of any differences that may arise in discussions at seminars or public lectures. His trainees are numerous, but it is noteworthy that none of them has achieved any level of recognizable status or power on their

own. They are transparently his disciples, easily recognized by their slavish emulation of the great master, and unable to enjoy any other training event in which they participate if it differs from their preconceived ideas of appropriateness.

While this is a somewhat extreme example of the supervisor who needs to be admired, there are other less drastic pitfalls into which such a supervisor may slip. The supervisor caught in such a trap is prone to try a variety of maneuvers calculated to maintain the illusion of complete agreement and superior knowledge. In the work with the supervisee, he may avoid any criticism of the student's work, relying instead on unconditional support, and the fantasy that one can transmit knowledge by a magical laying on of hands, or by keeping the student tied to his professional orbit.

Another version of this problem takes the form of the supervisor assuming an entertaining posture, providing ever more brilliant and witty interventions and avoiding the tedious and more mundane aspects of the work. A student objected loudly to her training director that her supervisor was spending the time telling her off-color jokes that were sexist and embarrassing. The supervisor felt that his primary skill as a supervisor was his capacity to charm and excite the student's spontaneity so that the student would intuitively learn to be "as competent and confident as I am, by relaxing and playing intellectually as I do." Just under the surface there seemed to exist the fantasy that the student's proximity to the supervisor would result in some transmission of information and skill.

The supervisor may share in a rebellious misalliance with the student against the institution, or against other supervisors. In doing so, he may lose the opportunity to deal with the student's neurotic tendency to split off one authority in order to defy another.

EXAMPLE: Mr. W. was a trainee on an inpatient unit that served a primarily adolescent population. In his first year of clinical training, he was easily persuaded by a group of these patients that it was in their interest to cancel the group therapy session in favor of a trip to the museum some few miles away. One patient was severely hurt when he bolted from the student's car, and the administration took harsh punitive action against the trainee. When he reported the ensuing disasters to his supervisor, the latter supported the student, feeling that the more traditional administration was taking an elitist position, and that he and his student had the correct attitude, since they were closer to the realities of these disadvantaged patients. This supervisor had long resented the lower status that his nondoctoral degree afforded him in a medical setting, and masked this resentment in a grandiose and unrealistic view of his superior competence compared to the doctors on the unit. Thus his unconscious identification with the underdog in the system impaired his judgment and blocked his ability to help his student learn from what turned out to be a major professional setback for this promising young man.

An overwhelming need to be admired can sometimes be cloaked in an overly humble and self-effacing stance that protects the supervisor from ever being accused of having been wrong or imprecise.

EXAMPLE: Dr. B. was assigned to supervise Dr. S., who came into the clinical field late, after years of experience as a pediatrician. Both members of the supervisory dyad were women of about the same age, and had the same numbers of years of professional experience. Dr. B. identified with her student, and projected her own fear of criticism on her; she then proceeded to treat Dr. S. as a colleague, with whom she would chat about the work in general collegial terms, missing the need for clear and precise supervision. The latter felt devalued and feared that her supervisor found her not worthy of training; she retaliated with a scathing criticism of the supervisor. Both women felt humiliated and defeated in the process, until the training director was able to help them sort out the confusion and misidentifications. The work then proceeded well.

2. THE NEED TO RESCUE

One of the givens among caretakers is that many enter the field in order to do for others that which they wish had been done for them at an earlier time in their lives. Another major given among professionals is that the patient must be protected from being used to unduly gratify the clinician's wishes. These same assumptions apply to supervisors in respect to their students. The affectional and collegial aspects of the supervisor/therapist relationship are one of the primary benefits for the supervisor, and a major motive for people to stay in the profession. A conscious acceptance of these impulses toward affiliation is needed to replace the somewhat guilty fantasies that interdependence continues to stimulate.

The supervisor whose own needs to be protective and needed are excessive distorts the work with the supervisee.

EXAMPLE: Dr. J. was assigned to supervise Dr. Y. in his work on an inpatient unit where the patients in his charge were in grave danger to themselves and to others. The supervisor insisted that the supervisee should call him each time any urgent situation arose, even if this should occur in the middle of the night. He insisted that the resident make no clinical decisions without consulting him first, and he would always offer to see the patient with the supervisee "should the latter feel the need to be accompanied." The resident resented this greatly, feeling that the supervisor did not trust him sufficiently, and that further, the supervisor was acting like an overprotective parent. Dr. J. felt that the student was greatly stressed by this case load, and should be supported every step of the way in order to survive this rotation. In contrast, the student expressed great distress. Upon discussing the situation, Dr. J. related that he had worked in a similar setting once, and been viciously attacked by a patient, with some resulting physical scars that lasted to the present. He attempted to restore his own self-esteem after the assault by being very careful to meet the student's needs. However, the press of his own unresolved anxiety interfered with his judgment of the student's neediness. In this case he needed to be needed much more than the student needed to be dependent. His overvigilance with his student was only secondarily related to the resident's circumstances, and he failed to see the latter's mounting resentment and passivity. The student was waiting eagerly for the end of this rotation, so that he could breathe again.

The need to be needed may result in giving the impression that the student's other supervisors were not really able to provide the same understanding or expertise. This undermining of other supervisors creates considerable tension for the student, and engenders a sense of disloyalty and suspicion in cases where the student is vulnerable enough to be pulled into an exclusive alliance of this sort.

EXAMPLE: Ms. D. was assigned a young student from a foreign country. She herself had emigrated some twenty years earlier, and clearly gave the student the message that people who had not shared this experience could not possibly help her, seeing that they were lacking in empathy and commonality of experience. This was especially problematic since they spoke the same foreign language, and the supervisor insisted on speaking this language in the supervision. Courtesy and a yearning for familiarity inhibited the student from trying to improve her knowledge of the local culture, and from making as strong a set of ties with other supervisors to benefit her fuure career growth.

3. THE NEED TO BE IN CONTROL

The work of supervision adds another layer of distance from the clinical situation, and increases the ambiguity that the supervisor must learn to tolerate. The supervisor's real power and control over the clinical situation are less immediate. For some this decrease in control generates competition with the supervisee, and/or a need to be in charge in a maladaptive way that contributes to supervisory impasse. The need to control can result in a competitive battle for control between supervisor and tainee.

For the novice supervisor, and for the more experienced one as well, issues of aggression, power, and competition are bound to surface and become a source of anxiety and gratification. On a conscious level, the supervisor has needs to feel in control, to be more competent than the supervisee, in order to be helpful and for his/her own sense of self-worth. If the supervisor experiences the supervisee as the validator of the former's sense of power and authority, there is a danger that the relationship will lapse into a struggle for dominance and control. Whether the supervisee is bright and very competent, or extraordinarily incompetent, the insecure supervisor is bound to feel threatened. Either he is about to be rendered useless, or the student is about to fail, and the rest of the world will hold the supervisor responsible. This combines with the less conscious issues of guilt and envy, with the result that the supervisor then responds to the student punitively or sadistically.

> *EXAMPLE:* Supervisor X. was assigned a supervisee, Dr. B., who was an extraordinarily brilliant young man who was publishing prolifically in his first year of residency, and showed no signs of slowing down in the second year, when the supervision took place. Dr. B. was engaged in a national research project and was clearly on his way to fame and acclaim. However, Dr. B. failed to come to supervision on time, and when he did come, he often explained that he hadn't time to prepare notes, or keep charts, since he was on an airplane last week, and so forth. Indeed, the administration had alerted the su-

pervisor to the fact that Dr. B. was not treating the expected number of cases, and was insulting to the support staff of the clinic when they resisted cancelling patient appointments for him. The supervisor was well aware that he envied Dr. B., that he feared his obvious scorn for the "soft" work of psychotherapy, and that he himself would rather cancel the supervision since he could hardly manage his feelings of competition with this wunderkind. Dr. X. judged correctly that the administration was very proud of having Dr. B. in their program, and feared that he might not have the support of the training director should he attempt to impose demands for more clinical commitment. The supervision floundered around the unspoken competition and rage until the final supervisory report, at which time the supervisor sent in a scathingly critical report of the resident, recommending that the resident not receive credit for that year, and generated huge levels of distress in the system. Upon investigation, it turned out that Dr. B. had in fact been presenting work to his other supervisors who had demanded such, and was acting out his "fast-track" anxiety with this supervisor, with whom he obviously shared a set of similar maladaptive defenses around competition and passive-aggressive control.

In the case above, the supervisor assumed a masochistically helpless posture with the student, and effectively abdicated appropriate levels of authority and control that the student needed for clinical growth and development.

Another form of impasse results when the supervisor, in an obsessive need to cover all the ground, launches a campaign to make the supervisee read massive quantities of relevant data and consider all alternatives, thereby discouraging the supervisee's ability for affective and intuitive learning.

EXAMPLE: Dr. W. was known in the system as a superior clinician, and a difficult supervisor. She regularly demanded fully typed process notes on each session, to be presented 24 hours before the supervision, along with detailed rationales for each intervention made by the student. Dr. L., her student, was an energetic, spontaneous, charming young man who was gifted poetically, and liked to take imaginary leaps that often led him to brilliant insights about a patient; sometimes, of course, his leaps caused him to fail badly. Both situations generated a stern response in the supervisor, who was alternatively envious and punitively critical of her supervisee. The more she demanded structure and precise reasoning, the more he felt his autonomy at risk, and the less he revealed to her in the supervisory hours. Eventually, he found himself inventing data for the supervision, and asked another supervisor for help. This time, the student was able to use the advice of the trusted mentor who suggested that he go back to Dr. W. and discuss the dilemma with her; together they worked out a reasonable compromise, and the year continued peacefully if not joyously.

4.   THE SUPERVISOR'S NEED FOR COMPETITION

If a supervisor is naturally competitive and ambitious he may feel tempted to engage in activities that maintain clear superiority over the student. He may overwhelm the trainee with data, or solve the problem rather than let the student struggle to find his own solutions. He may dazzle with complicated and esoteric insights, or undercut the student's creativity by ignoring or taking credit for it. Sometimes the supervisor may work with a student who is indeed much like a younger and somewhat idealized version of himself in an earlier time. The former may be so identified with the student, and so vicariously committed to this student's excelling over his colleagues that the student's reality is compromised in favor of the supervisor's competitive instincts and dreams of glory.

Some of the more difficult competitive situations arise when a supervisor is supervising across disciplines, or across gender, or race, or age barriers. These situations are extremely painful because the underlying issues are rarely addressed openly in training systems, and remain the source of shame and confusion in both parties to the supervision. More will be said about bias in Chapter Seven, but it is worth noting that competition is one of many complicating issues in this dyad, and often is mistaken for prejudice on the part of the supervisor, rather than acknowledged and dealt with on its own terms.

> *EXAMPLE:* Mr. G. is an extremely competent social worker, an expert in the field of family therapy; he is the primary supervisor for this modality in his training center, which is in a medical setting. In supervising Dr. F., he found himself critical, irritable, and impatient with her; she responded by refusing to be supervised by "a social worker," and stated that she felt demeaned. When Mr. G. was consulted he admitted that he had in fact been short with her, in a way that was unusual for him. He further allowed that he was quite impressed with her natural talent for the work, and by her formidable intellectual abilities. He was openly envious of her plans to take over a family treatment program in a nearby hospital at the completion of her residency; this was not made any easier by her bragging to him that she would be earning three times his salary in her first year out of training!
>
> Their conflict was open to huge areas of misinterpretation: She felt that he was chauvinistic, controlling, and resentful of women in positions of power; he felt that she was scornful of his professional identity, that she resisted learning from him by refusing to let him in on her interviews with the families she treated, and was flaunting her higher status. They sought consultation with a senior supervisor and sorted out their difficulties. At present, he is employed by her hospital to consult on the ward which she directs; they are in the process of co-authoring a journal article, and are clearly enjoying their new collegiality.

5. THE NEED TO BE LOVED

It is a given that the patient must be protected from being used for the gratification of the therapist; the paucity of theory about supervision has led to some direct extrapolation of this concept to the supervisory relationship with some ensuing confusion and anxiety that sets the stage for potential impasse. As stated earlier, it is my contention that the affectional and collegial aspects of the supervisor/supervisee relationship are primary benefits for the supervisor, and a major motive for people to stay in the profession. An example of the denial of this reality is expressed by Chessick (6) who speaks with some embarrassment about the secondary gains for the supervisor, such as the need for company, for emotional relief from the deprivation of direct patient care and the stresses this produces on one's personal life. The supervisor who is lonely, or angry, or depressed, and feels constrained from thinking that the work with the supervisees offers some appropriate relief is in danger of acting out these very needs in ways that are inappropriate. The supervisor who is aware of the need to be loved and gratified by the supervisee is in a position to keep careful check on the management of his object hunger, and to keep the affection in the relationship at levels consistent with the supervisory boundaries and goals.

EXAMPLE 2: Dr. L. is a young staff clinician employed by the same department in which she recently completed her training. She has been pressed into supervising students who are one or two years her junior, and while she is very anxious and unready to supervise, she confided in a former supervisor that she dared not refuse the assignment, because to do so would be to seriously diminish her value to the department. Her perception may have been quite accurate, which added to the pressure to perform at extremely high levels of competence that this woman always feels, whether ready or not. She is also at the point in her life where her primary personal and developmental goal is the formation of an intimate relationship; she is conscious of her wish to have a child before she is much older, and is concerned with how to do so while balancing the pressures of an academic career in a highly competitive setting. She was assigned a supervisee who is two years her junior, a handsome and charming married man who is a promising clinician who has the stated goals of becoming an analyst. Dr. L. was very worried that she had little to offer this student as a supervisor; in addition, she felt very attracted to him sexually, and was on the verge of becoming involved in an affair that would obviously replace the therapeutic relationship. When her own analyst questioned the wisdom of this arrangement, she came asking a trusted mentor for help. Her former supervisor was able to sort out with her her avoidance of the supervisory tension, and her personal interference with the situation; Dr. L. was able then to proceed with the work of supervision in a way that proved very satisfactory to both.

EXAMPLE 2: Dr. R. is an analyst and a senior supervisor in a setting that has recently shifted from a more psychodynamic to a more biologic treatment philosophy. Within two years, he went from being voted the most popular supervisor of the year, to having a couple of unused supervisory hours. He understandably felt unloved, unappreciated, and diminished, at a time of life when his wife was struggling with a terminal illness. This set in motion a situation in which Dr. R. became very concerned with "converting" students to his point of view, and insisting that his students agree that the biologic method was ridiculous and harmful to patients. Efforts on his students' part to engage him in a dialogue, or to avoid arguments about the position were countered with jokes or sarcasm; the supervisees would end up feeling mocked and disrespected; they retaliated by making fun of his mannerisms. They felt torn between their commitment to the departmental policy, and his obvious need for them to agree with him and value his position above all others. He frequently invited them to his home, and increasingly looked to them for social contact and reassurance. A vicious circle was created, in which they began to avoid him, and he, feeling even more unloved, vigorously renewed his stance. Eventually, he began to miss supervisory appointments, or to convert the supervisory hour into a visit in which he and the supervisee would chat about the doings of the local psychoanalytic institute. Unfortunately, his contribution as a supervisor of psychotherapy was mainly lost, and he moved to the position of a friendly elder in the department, whom people loved but did not choose as a supervisor. This was a great loss, since his profound wealth of competence and wisdom failed to be nurtured and maintained. Eventually he was dropped from the supervisor roster, to the unfortunate diminishment of all parts of the program.

EXAMPLE 3: Dr. C. is a very sweet, pleasant clinician who is sought after by supervisees because she is supportive and reassuring. Ms. R. was assigned to her for supervision as a first year trainee. When Ms. R. began to treat a very needy and demanding patient, she felt herself disgusted with the patient, and reported to her supervisor that she felt the patient inappropriate for psychotherapy; at best, she felt that the patient was hopelessly pathological, and could make no progress. Dr. C. felt that the student was in need of her unconditional positive regard, and would do nothing to dispute the trainee's attitude toward the patient. She felt that the trainee needed a friend most of all in this early part of her training, and refused to "pressure the student," lest the student feel that Dr. C. was unloving toward her. The projection of the supervisor's own needs to be loved was a chronic problem for her and for her students. While Ms. R. felt loved by Dr. C. and loved her in return, she began the next year with another supervisor only to find that she had been deprived of some very important training, not the least of which was the capacity to deal with the narcissistic injuries that are a normal part of the learning regression. Ms. R. felt humiliated by her new supervisor's criticism and struggled to learn from a less vulnerable stance what her beloved supervisor had failed to teach her.

6. THE NEED TO WORK THROUGH UNRESOLVED
   PRIOR CONFLICTS IN THE SUPERVISOR'S
   OWN TRAINING EXPERIENCE

Another problem arises from the paucity of dialogue and training in the field of supervision. People enter with models from their own experience as supervisees, with little capacity to assess how much of what they experienced was due to the failures or brilliance of their prior supervisors, and how much of their memory is tainted by the regressive transferences that occur in any normal supervision. There is no public arena for sorting out fantasy from reality and the distortions remain secret and charged with leftover feelings of distress or idealization. These same supervisors form the supervisory introjects for the beginning supervisor. To the extent that they experienced conflict with prior supervisors that remained unresolved, they will run the risk of distorting their own professional development, in an unconscious variant of the repetition compulsion.

EXAMPLE 1: Dr. S. was supervising Dr. A., new to the field. Dr. S. recalled that her first supervisor tended to criticize harshly and to demand unusual levels of competence; she resolved never to criticize a student for being inept in the first year of training. Whenever Dr. A. presented his doubts about his performance in a particular situation, Dr. S. would rush to reassure him that he was doing fine, and indeed was expecting too much of himself. This process continued and escalated, until Dr. S. complained to her that he felt severely criticized for his wish to excel! The supervisor was horrified to find that she had replicated just what she had sought to avoid, and was able to make the necessary adjustment when she realized the source of her overdetermined "reassurance" of a student who didn't need or want this approach.

EXAMPLE 2: Dr. J. is a very popular supervisor, who had enjoyed and benefited from a wealth of excellent supervisors in his own training. In particular, he had worked with a supervisor whom he idealized and emulated for a number of years. However, he was now developing his own supervisory identity, and felt that his autonomy required that he repudiate his former supervisor's teaching stance. He was assigned a student who happened to work with both Dr. J. and his formerly idealized supervisor. Thus, whenever the student reported a case, Dr. J. tended to tell the student that while the other supervisor might do thus and such, he felt differently, and would advise the student to follow his lead instead. This generated confusion in the student, who felt that both supervisors were valuable, and couldn't understand the constant contrasting of positions by Dr. J. He began to feel that Dr. J. was not to be trusted, and withdrew from the relationship. Dr. J., uninformed as to the reasons, was unable to deal with this, since the student felt too unsafe to confront the supervisor with his feelings of divided loyalties, and the situation remained checkmated for the year.

7. SPILLOVER FROM STRESS IN THE PERSONAL OR
   PROFESSIONAL LIFE OF THE SUPERVISOR
   (TRUE SUPERVISORY COUNTERTRANSFERENCE)

If the supervisor is experiencing distress in his own life that is creating overwhelming tension, the chances are great that this will seep into the work of supervision. If the supervisor is conscious of it, even when the problem is acute, it rarely results in impasse. Impasse around this area results from unconscious intrusion into the work, from unresolved conflicts that are stimulated in the supervisor by the circumstances of his life. In the example of the supervisor whose needs for love were related to the impending loss of his wife, the problems in the supervision arose not from his awareness of his loneliness, but rather from his irritability and resultant criticism of the student, which he failed to recognize as related to the losses in his own life. If the supervisor is chronically restricted in these ways, then the work with the supervisees will result in perennial difficulties.

EXAMPLE: Dr. B. was a bright, competent supervisor who liked working with students, especially beginners. He tended to select his supervisees carefully, and the work went well. With a change in administration, the supervisees were given much more autonomy in selecting the supervisors—a real reversal of the process of matching. Dr. B. was then in the position of working with some students whose character type was very problematic to him. In particular, his work with Ms. V. began in conflict, and never proceeded beyond that point. He felt that she was inadequately trained, he held her in some intellectual contempt, and generally made the situation miserable for her and for himself. When she protested, he insisted that she take up the problem with her therapist, and then get back to him and tell him when she had done so. The director of training intervened, and Dr. B. announced that it was his opinion that Ms. V's hysterical thinking was clearly inadequate, and that he felt insulted that he had been asked to supervise such an inept student. When this scenario recurred twice in the ensuing years, it became clear that this supervisor had a limited range of competence, and he was assigned carefully chosen trainees thereafter; he continued to function adequately within his range.

8. TENSION BETWEEN THE SUPERVISOR AND
   THE ADMINISTRATION OF THE INSTITUTION

Where the supervisor feels unsupported, uncherished, or underpaid by the institution, there is serious potential for these conflicts to spill over into the supervisory hour. He may resist writing adequate supervisory reports for the training committee, bring resentment into the supervisory interchange, or somehow expect the student to make up for the sins of the system. In any event, the ombudsman function that the supervisor should provide for negotiating between the student and all other parties is virtually lost. In fact, the supervisor may unconsciously encourage acting-out against the institution by ignoring the student, who may take on an insufficient work load, or adhere too casually to administrative policy, billing procedures, and so forth. Caught in a demoralizing bind, the student may withdraw in disillusion or seek more peaceful alternative areas of specialization for reasons other than his best interest or future career directions.

Impasse sometimes occurs in ways that remain impossible to analyze and remedy. The common assumption is that the dyad is stimulating some powerful transferential and countertransferential reactions in one another, and the only real solution is to reassign the student, and to do whatever is possible to assure the supervisor of his/her continued value to the institution.

Suggestions to facilitate the resolution of problems in supervision

Regularly scheduled meetings of psychotherapy supervisors are a powerful resource for the resolution of impasse. These contacts encourage a dialogue among supervisors in which they can share supervisory tactics and experiences, and seek help from one another in difficult cases.

The attitude of the director of training and of the administration must be that the supervision of psychotherapy is a highly valued activity, and is publicly recognized as such. Presentations at grand rounds around the topic of supervision, or a presentation of a taped supervisory hour are ways in which the process is made public and less mysterious to both supervisees and trainees. Early in the training year, students should be instructed on how to use supervision optimally. Further, there must be a consultant who can be available to the supervisor or the supervisee when they arrive at some stalemate. This could be the director of training, but ideally it would be a senior supervisor who is assigned this role in the department, and who can function as a troubleshooter and ombudsman in the supervisory system.

The administration should provide supervisors who represent a variety of perspectives, who are men and women of a broad enough age range to span all the developmental stages, and who can interact with the supervisees from a richly heterogeneous set of assumptions and strengths.

Finally, the problem of impasse must be faced by the training committee in a way that deals realistically and compassionately with all the concerned parties. Efforts must be made to reduce impasse situations by training young clinicians to supervise, and to develop fresh theory to inform the field of supervision in the future.

References

1. Wallerstein, R. Personal communication, 1979.
2. Jones, E. The God Complex, in *Essays in Applied Psychoanalysis.* London: The Hogarth Press, 1951 (II:244).
3. Mehlman, R. Becoming and Being a Psychotherapist: the Problem of Narcissism, *Int. J. Psychiatry,* 1974, V3., 125–141.
4. Semrad, E. *Teaching Psychotherpay of Psychotic Patients.* N.Y.: Grune Stratton, 1969.
5. Searles, H. F. The Informational Value of the Supervisor's Emotional Experience, *Psychiatry,* 1955, 18, p. 135–146.
6. Chessick, R. *Why Psychotherapists Fail.* N.Y.: Science House, 1971.

7

Some Special
Circumstances
of Supervision

The past two decades have seen some exciting expansions in the clinical arena, evidenced by the multiplicity of treatment modalities that have emerged and by the large variety of people who are seeking clinical training in these modalities. The traditional training institutions are now working with applicants who are often different in age or background from those who had previously trained in these settings.

While credentialling and licensing bodies have sought to ensure some measure of professional standards and quality control, to date they have offered minimally useful guidelines for training clinicians in the day-to-day work with their patients. The supervisor is more responsible than ever to see to the clinical development of his trainee, and to rise to the challenge of changing clinical times and mores.

Most supervisor's work has consisted of a more or less implicit reiteration of their own training experience, but most mid-life or older supervisors were trained prior to the latest professional developments. The need to think anew about the supervisory process offers an opportunity to step out of the more traditional definitions of supervision and to expand the view of the work with students. But supervisors are not immune to the confusion and anxiety that accompany revolutionary change, however much they may approve of the direction of the change. This chapter is directed toward clarifying some of the confusion by delineating some of the specific changes in the field, and examining their impact on supervisors of psychotherapy.

Supervising modalities other than individual therapy

Psychodynamic psychotherapy emerged from the field of psychoanalysis, with its emphasis on the psychoanalytic dyad. Prior to the last twenty years, most schools of therapy emulated the one patient, one analyst model, which was then replicated in the one student, one supervisor training model. With the emergence of group therapy and then family therapy, the field of systems theory began to address the power of the group and the forces that can be observed and harnessed when the members of a group are worked with as a whole. This shift toward treating groups of patients together was buttressed by the demands for delivery of health care to burgeoning numbers of patients in our clinics and by the increased cost of individual psychotherapy, putting the latter out of the reach of a great many people who needed and continue to need treatment.

In order to replicate the experience and theory of group psychotherapy for training clinicians in that modality, many supervisors now work with more than one student at the same time. This serves to familiarize the trainees with the theoretical and practical techniques of a model in which they may have little or no personal experience either as clinicians or as patients.

In fact, major supervisory innovations have emerged that involve a dramatically different role for the supervisor. Often supervisors function as senior clinicians working hand in hand with the trainee to lead a group or intervene with a family. Sometimes the supervisor observes the work of the clinician-in-training though a one-way mirror, or allows the supervisee to observe him work with patients. Other supervisors may remain more traditionally removed from the treatment hour, but attempt to provide a climate that allows for a modification of the parallel process; he may insist on supervising group therapy by including several trainees in the same supervisory hour, thus modeling the techniques of group work. Another may supervise family therapy by inviting the learner to reflect on his family of origin as a point of comparison and contrast with the patient family, again adding a powerful experimental and modeling component to the learning. Another may employ psychodrama to help the student "live" in the patient's feelings and dilemmas.

These new departures are an excellent opportunity to model thoughtful flexibility of technique, and to open a dialogue with the student for exploring both theoretical and personal preferences and biases. They move both parties away from the unchallenged "givens" of training institutions, and offer fresh opportunities for research and further development.

Supervising across professional disciplines

One of the enriching innovations in clinical centers is the increasing acceptability of supervisors from many professional disciplines. In part this is related to the increasing awareness that psychotherapy skills cut across professional disciplines. It is also true that with the larger range of treatment modalities, supervisors have tended to be identified as specialists rather than generalists. In addition, no therapist, even a generalist, can be fully expert in all current modalities. Therefore, it has become the practice in more sophisticated centers of training to utilize supervisors according to their expertise rather than their professional training. Psychologists, psychiatrists, social workers and others all participate as supervisors in increasingly significant numbers. As supervisors gain more experience working with allied colleagues, new and unfamiliar variables enter the training situation.

When a supervisor from one discipline supervises someone

from another field, he is apt to encounter some attitudes, skills, and traits that are unfamiliar and potentially confusing to work with. Some specific responses have been reinforced in the training of psychiatrists that are unfamiliar to psychologists, and so forth. For example, medical students are trained to make spot judgments and action-oriented decisions. Psychologists, on the other hand, are often trained to contemplate all details surrounding the issue and to examine statistical probability before making a final judgment about a situation. Social workers and psychiatric nurses have often been trained to attend to the comfort of the patient and to move as quickly as possible to relieve distress emanating from external sources as a first treatment maneuver. These assumptions constitute the cultural mores that are agreed upon and practiced as a matter of course. A psychologist-supervisor, however, may be at a loss to understand the ready tendency of a young psychiatric resident to act in a way that the supervisor may judge to be rash and presumptive, when the resident is simply following the mores of medicine. Similarly, a social worker supervisor who is paired with a psychology intern may be distressed by the apparent passivity or callousness of the psychologist-in-training toward the patient's pain, whereas the trainee may feel that to move with insufficient data constitutes careless management of the situation and is potentially dangerous to the patient.

These professional assumptions are rarely conscious, and they are not often discussed in the supervision; when the work of supervision begins to falter, it would be very useful to step back and examine which of the differing perspectives are based in the professional culture of the supervisor and the student, and which represent a real failure in the training situation. Especially at the time of negotiating a supervisory contract, some attention to differing backgrounds of training can facilitate the capacity of each member of the supervisory dyad to see the world more empathically from the other's perspective. If the supervisor feels that the clinician needs to change his technique or his perspective, at least both parties can be more sensitive to the enormity of the task.

Supervising across age barriers

The feminist movement has generated major changes in the professional culture that have serious implications for the supervision of clinicians of both sexes, and all ages. Some of these social and psychological changes affect the type of therapist now found in training. Older women have come to recognize their intellectual and professional ambitions and have been encouraged to pursue their careers outside the traditional arenas of home, children, and church. Many others who were employed at lower level work have recognized some of the cultural and personal limitations and rebelled, choosing instead to pursue long abandoned dreams of an autonomous career. A host of other women have reentered the work force with more ambivalence after a divorce or widowhood and hold very mixed feelings about their current status. Men too have found encouragement to change jobs at mid-life, or to pursue clinical careers as an economic solution in an era where academic and research money is scarce.

All these groups enter the supervisory situation with a long history of attitudes and expectations that may intrigue and intimidate the supervisor, especially when he may be fifteen or twenty years their younger. The supervisor who is an age contemporary but with some 15 or more years of clinical experience must exert great tact in order to mediate the painful comparisons of professional status and power with the student. A supervisor who is very secure in professional and personal terms may find this situation one which represents the best ideals of androgogic learning. However, these changes may also generate difficulties in the supervisory relationship, primarily due to empathic barriers that can loom large in the heated emotional atmosphere of supervision. Some of these barriers originate with the supervisor, who may have a number of unresolved conflicts about age and gender. For example, the female professional who has made compromises in her personal life to pursue her professional career may look with some envy at her female student who enjoyed the prerogatives of a more traditional female role, or at her male student whom she may perceive as having had more freedom to choose a career direction. She may now feel that she has to prove the value of her life choices by performing superbly with her student, and may feel very badly indeed should she or her student fail.

EXAMPLE: Dr. S. was a very promising supervisor, three years out of training. She was assigned Dr. E. as a psychotherapy student for the year. Dr. E. had been a clergyman and at age fifty was changing from a career as a pastoral counselor to that of a clinical psychologist. Dr. S. was 34 years old at the time, very interested in being a fine supervisor, and was very anxious about her assignment. She expressed this only indirectly, raising frequent questions about Dr. E's motivation for learning a new way to practice, or about his capacity to fit in with the other trainees in his class. Dr. E., on his part, felt that Dr. S. was very critical of him, and tried to prove himself by talking to her often about his prior successes, which were impressive. He would further enrage her by commenting on how pretty she looked and felt hurt about what he considered her coldness. To add to their confusion, they had come from very different geographic and cultural settings; he grew up in the south, where his courtly manners were the rule; she came from a sophisticated urban center where her professional stance was judged as appropriately reserved, if a bit stiff. She was also a dedicated feminist and resented what she saw as his unconscious jockeying for power in his "good old days" stories. They struggled along with increasing levels of tension until she presented the situation in a supervision seminar. She felt ashamed of her wish to humiliate her student, was aware that she wished he would disappear, and feared that her own capacity to supervise was limited compared to that of her colleagues and her former supervisors whom she wished to emulate. A colleague in the seminar reminisced about her difficulties in working with a senior male supervisor at a time in her life when she had just immigrated to this country, managed to get licensed, and begun a practice. She felt very vulnerable to this supervisor's barely masked chauvinism and greatly regretted that she had never had the courage to discuss it with him directly, since she had come to admire his skill as a clinician and teacher in the community. This began a dialogue about the limits of supervisory empathy that was very helpful to Dr. S. She spoke frankly to Dr. E. about the problem. He was able to articulate his needs for her approval and the work proceeded splendidly.

The above example is clearly one in which Dr. E's transference fantasies and distortions toward his supervisor were generating hostile/seductive feelings and behaviors. Since transference by definition is unconscious, he had no way of perceiving or understanding the inappropriateness of his stance. Dr. S. was also reacting from her own countertransference needs, having to do with her ancient struggle in finding a place for herself in the eyes of her powerful but rejecting father.

An important postscript came some months later when Dr. E. admitted to his supervisor that he was, in fact, in trouble with his colleagues, who found him arrogant and stubborn. She was able to help him become aware of how they might be feeling and why, given her earlier distress in the work with him. He was able to accept her help and avoided what was about to become a training failure for him.

The fantasied distortions of this supervisory dyad provided the background for the difficulties in the real supervisory relationship, and exaggerated an understandably tense situation to the point of some distress. Fortunately, the supervisor's courage in presenting this problem in the seminar and her willingness to examine her own response with an open mind enabled her to free herself and her student from the ghosts of the past so that the present could be dealt with gracefully.

Supervising across gender barriers

The women's movement has sensitizied clinicians to the fact that gender bias is ubiquitous and affects all levels of personal interactions. Supervisory relationships are vulnerable to blind spots related to gender, but also provide an arena for consciousness raising that can make a major contribution toward a more enlightened development of theory, training, and clinical intervention.

There is a special need to reconsider some of the sociopolitical assumptions about female psychology given the distortions that were offered as fact just a few decades ago by the leading theoreticians in the field of mental health, e.g., Freud (1) and Jung (2). This bias was expressed by Bruno Bettelheim (3), who was later to pubish specific advice to mothers (!). Bettleheim said "As much as women want to be good scientists and engineers, they want first and foremost to be womanly companions of men and to be mothers" (p. 18). The heavy loading of these theoretical assumptions permeated the professional culture in which most currently practicing clinicians and supervisors were trained, and must be carefully reexamined in the work with our supervisees, lest the distortions continue in their work with their patients.

In the more common situation in psychiatry and clinical psychology, the supervisor is male, and the patient is apt to be female. The supervisor then has the task of expanding the male or female trainee's empathy for the patient. This places the supervisor in a position where he must especially be vigilant about his own gender assumptions, as well as that which is built into the clinical theory. Of course the same is true for the female supervisor, who may be more sensitizied to the bias issues, but may harbor political stances that could be clouding her vision of the clinical situation or of the trainee's needs just as much. The supervisor bears the greater burden of responsibility here, especially since there is a reluctance to discuss gender bias in most training settings. This is true in part because of an overall cultural blindness to its influence in the professional sphere and in part in deference to the boundaries of supervision and a wish not to skew the view of the patient's dilemma too far away from the intrapsychic and the interpersonal to the political sphere. If the male supervisor carries the special burden of self-examination in his work with his trainees, the female supervisor is also faced with a difficult task when she tries to address distortions or omissions that indicate bias in her male student; she must confront him on a politically and narcissistically sensitive issue while remaining respectful and empathic lest the student experience humiliation in lieu of learning.

EXAMPLE: Dr. A. began the year with his female supervisor, Dr. W., by saying that he had a patient to present but he was not optimistic about the work since the patient was an older woman of fifty-three who showed little capacity for insight, preferring instead to rail at him for not understanding her plight. He and his former (male) supervisor, Dr. J. had decided that he should send her to medication clinic as soon as he could find a more interesting patient to present in supervision. In fact, he admitted his commitment to work with the patient in psychotherapy was based on his wish to work with Dr. W., and he had no other patient to present who was not already being supervised.

The supervisor was immediately confronted with a number of dilemmas. She admired Dr. J., and was not about to ignore his recommendations; she was also aware of his very traditional theoretical position, so she was not willing to accept his word uncritically. The student was clearly more ambivalent than he could recognize about dismissing the patient, since many more patients were available in the clinic if he really wanted to choose another. Finally, she needed to deal with her own identification with the patient, who was a contemporary and who was being written off as hopeless. All of these factors tended to confuse the more objective evaluation of the patient.

Dr. W. helped the student become aware of the potential biases in the situation—from him, from her, from Dr. J., and not the least of all, from the patient herself. They decided to reevaluate, re-diagnose, and re-formulate the case with all the above in mind. A careful formulation suggested that the case was worth a try. The work proceeded quite well—until the supervision came to a close. On follow-up, it was noted that the patient dropped out of treatment at the end of the year, leaving the supervisor to contemplate the influence of the supervisory relationship on the treatment once again!

The examples above contrast sharply with more traditional role and gender bias as represented in the following example in which the work foundered on those shoals.

EXAMPLE: Dr. D., a young analyst, was assigned a new psychology interne to supervise. Ms. A. had just begun her clinical work, and was anxiously and awkwardly presenting her first patient. After listening for a few minutes, he picked up the newspaper and began to look through it, urging her to continue, and assuring her that he would tell her when she got to an interesting part.

She felt his scorn, and tolerated it for a long time since she shared his opinion of her work, and was intimidated by his rank and clear influence in the training center. She also had no prior supervisory experience and was not in a position to make an informed criticism of his technique, even had she dared to do so.

This process lasted six months before she found the courage to protest and to demand that he put down the newspaper, only to be told how cute she was when she got angry. Learning stopped at this point, and while she compliantly came to the supervision hour, they mostly chatted about his cases. Many years later, she learned that Dr. D. lost his first born child that year, and was disabled with grief. Had they been able to discuss this, or to find a consultant to respond to the impasse, supervision might have turned into a warm and creative alliance. As it was they both succumbed to traditional defensive postures and the supervision failed.

This chapter has considered some of the special circumstances of supervision that have to do with changes in the field and in the culture surrounding the practice of psychotherapy. Alterations in tradition tend to illuminate areas of bias, and only a very few are described here. Issues of racial and cultural bias need to be carefully sorted out, as do those of geographic and class differences between supervisor and trainee. The supervisor's age, background, theoretical stance and personal life are all contributors to the situation.

Finally, the supervisor and the student need to recognize the limits of the empathic capacity, and to make peace with some of these limitations. A failure to do so can catch the supervisor and the clinican in what Jones (4) referred to as "God complex"—an arrogant and grandoise countertransferential stance far removed from intimacy with the patient.

An appropriate humility encourages an honest and realistic appraisal of the parties involved, and circumscribes the limits of any one person to enter another's experience, however much one may wish to do so. The supervisor's admission of his own struggles and limitations can encourage the student to explore his own boundaries with equal honesty.

References

1. See Freud, S. New Introductory Lectures. New York: W. W. Norton Co., Inc., 1933.
2. See also Jung, C. *Contributions to Analytic Psychology.* New York: Harcourt Brace, 1928.
3. Bettlehelm, B. The commitment required for young women entering

a scientific profession in present day American society. Presented at the Mass. Institute of Technology Symposium on American Women in Science and Engineering. Cambridge, Mass., May 21–23, 1965; p. 18.

4. Jones, E. The god complex. In *Essays in Applied Psychoanalysis*. London: Horgarth Press, 1951, Vol. 2, p. 244.

8

The Supervisory Encounter

The anatomy of a supervisory encounter bears strong resemblance to that of the therapeutic encounter with the patient. There is a logical predictable unfolding of process and content that a trained clinician can hear imbedded in the verbal exchanges. The supervisor listens to the trainee with an ear open to process (Why is he reporting this at this time, and in this way?), and to the content (What does this tell us about the patient's diagnosis or the student's fund of knowledge?). He then helps the student to hear and understand meanings that the latter is only vaguely aware of communicating, and offers support and insight that encourage the supervisee to bear the anxiety that is necessary for further growth. The supervisor's clear thinking and theoretical soundness serve to calm the clinician's anxiety and provide intellectual depth that helps organize the plethora of emotional stimuli generated by the contact with the patient. In effect, the supervisor "heals" the student's clinical vulnerability and leaves him with a stronger clinical ego.

Apart from a general attitude of empathy and respect, the primary channel for the supervisor's influence on this dual "healing" is the parallel process. This assumes that the student will select from the patient's hour some areas of conflict in which he unconsciously merges with the patient, and will present this material for the supervisor to "cure". The supervisor who is tuned in to this parallel level of communication will speak about the patient hour while being fully aware that he is simultaneously speaking to the clinician about himself. The partial merger connects the unconscious of the three immediate parties to the supervision—the supervisor, the therapist, and the patient. The supervisor who is available and willing to immerse himself in this unconscious pool contributes immensely to the reservoir of available ego for the other two. To the extent that this occurs, the entire relationship models the treatment, and the parallel process is taken advantage of for the clinician's learning and the patient's best interest. To maintain the accuracy of this hall of mirrors effect the supervisor must remain aware that there are few possibilities for "off the cuff" behaviors with the student; any carelessness is apt to find its counterpart in the latter's work with the patient. One problem is that this consciousness of all levels of impact imposes constraints on the spontaneity of the supervisory hour. This is unfortunate because many supervisors supervise in order to enjoy a greater freedom from the constraints of doing psychotherapy. It is to be hoped that this restriction on freedom is compensated for by the growing perception of one's effectiveness as a mentor.

What happens in the supervisory encounter?

The overall parameters of the supervisory work can be divided into three main segments: Beginning phase supervision, mid-phase, and end phase. Each of these phases encompasses some specific content and process aspects, which can be predicted and addressed in an orderly way. Both the process and content of each stage can be defined as follows:

Beginning phase supervision

Process

The attitude with which the supervisor greets and establishes contact with the student plays a paramount part in the overall atmosphere of the work. A serious, tactful, and respectful attitude toward the trainee, and attention to his vulnerable self-esteem will permit the learning alliance to be more easily established. This learning alliance has its counterpart in the narcissistic alliance that must be established with the patient before any change can be expected to occur. It is also true that in the early weeks of supervision, the trainee may plunge into a learning regression related to finding out how much there is to be known and understood. For people with prior clinical experience there is the dismaying awareness of how much needs to be unlearned.

An attitude of nonjudgmental curiosity about the problems in the early work can be very reassuring to the student, and encourages the same attitude of nonjudgmental analysis in the psychotherapy. It is also here that the younger supervisor needs the support and perspective of a more experienced colleague in order to see this regression as a necessary and positive signal of the student's availability for new learning.

Content

The content of the beginning phase of supervision includes the contract, the development of a learning diagnosis, and the beginning of the evaluation process.

THE CONTRACT

The supervisor and trainee are engaged in an implicit contract that is best made explicit. This contract defines the parameters of the work. For example, this is when they will usually agree about which patient will be presented and which will not be discussed with this particular supervisor. Most supervisors request that the student present a patient only to one supervisor at a time. It is here too that supervisors will tend to explain their philosophy of treatment. The method of presentation is contracted at this time, i.e., process notes, verbatim accounts, tape recordings, or other. The supervisor should let the student know when he plans to be away, and inquire about the other's vacation plans. As hour should be fixed, with some discussion about punctuality and location.

PAST HISTORY AND SUPERVISION

Both the trainee and the supervisor will profit from some exchange about their prior experiences with and expectations of supervision. It is especially useful to be aware of the positive encounters with prior supervisors for both to have some idea of their professional ego-ideals. This may also be a time for the trainee to share some painful supervisory memories, although some caution must be exercised here lest the shared anxiety of the student and the supervisor cause them to collude in a distortion and splitting of good/bad supervisory imagos. The point is for them to be aware of what are the more positive, and the more painful memories, and to be guided by history in predicting and adjusting the course of the work.

LEARNING DIAGNOSIS

There will begin to emerge a profile of the student in terms of how he learns best, to use a fairly simple example. The more obsessional student may need to calm his anxiety with readings, while the more hysterical student may be made all the more anxious when handed a sheaf of journal articles. The supervisor, too, has a preferred supervising style, and this is the time to explicate the rationale for this to the student. Here, too, the life stage imperatives can begin to be addressed. The trainee who goes home to a new baby is hardly in much of a position to want to do much reading but may be encouraged by the supervisor's empathic recall of some of the ways he coped with the demands of a young family.

A careful discussion of the above factors will lead to the beginnings of a learning plan for the year. To the extent that this plan is written out in behavioral terms, this will form a baseline from which the two can assess progress or lack of it at the time of supervisory evaluation. For example, if the dyad agree that the trainee needs to learn how to "listen with the third ear" [Reik (1)] to the patient and to distinguish between regression and fixation, and perhaps to learn how to evolve a dynamic formulation of the case, then these can become specific goals for the year. At the mid-year evaluation they can re-examine the learning plan (each should have a copy) and write an evaluation that includes degrees of progress toward these goals. This also serves as a springboard to discuss the limits of confidentiality in supervision, and the supervisor's potential ombudsman role for the trainee with the administration. This contracting is a critical and sensitive part of the supervisory agreement. The student needs to know that the supervisor has allegiance to the whole mental health care system, including the supervisee's interest, which he sees as integral with the care of the patient and maintenance of quality control of the institution. Further, the supervisor must clarify that he will be in communication with the director of training and other administrators, and will be available to facilitate communication between the supervisee and these people. In case of difficulties, the supervisor will make what information he has available to the student and to the training director, and will support the system's standards as best he can, consistent with ethical and prudent patient care and the student's best interest.

This is also the time for the supervisor to make clear any firmly held convictions that will apply to the work. The capacity to be and to appear objective will never be so available as in the beginning phase of the supervision and the supervisor would do well to seize the opportunity to broach a potentially delicate topic from a more generalizable stance. For example, this is the time when a supervisor might state a strong belief that any serious clinician should be in psychotherapy for a protracted period of time in order to be able to separate self-interest from patient generated impulses. To say so now, before the situation deepens, is to say to the student, in effect, that this is not a personal criticism, since the two are still virtual strangers.

Mid-phase supervision

The majority of contact between the supervisor and student at this stage will be concentrated on incorporation, identification, and integration.

These three processes will be repeated again and again in the course of serious training in a learning helix that brings the student into deeper levels of clinical competence and confidence in his capacity to practice autonomously. This repeating process is analogous to the concept of working through in therapy. It is here that the characterological patterns of the student will be illuminated, and here also where they can be altered if need be.

Incorporation

Given an adequate learning alliance, the new trainee will begin uncritically to mimic the supervisor. Sometimes the hour is replete with verbal expressions that the supervisor will recognize with alarming familiarity. At other times the student will report that "I did exactly what you said, and it was astounding what happened!" This idealization will also come crashing down periodically when the blind mimicry fails to impress the patient. The supervisor may feel flattered, embarrassed, or even guilty that he may be overly controlling and influencing the student too strongly. While all the above may be true, it is also true that a

126

trainee normally goes through a sorcerer's apprentice phase of learning, especially if the supervisor is highly valued. It is important for the supervisor to tolerate a certain amount of this mimicry without comment or criticism, since the student is still vulnerable to shame at this stage. Eventually, if the supervisor avoids too much didactic teaching, and stays with a more Socratic method, the trainee will begin to look with greater discrimination at the supervisor's position. In fact, toward the end of the incorporation phase, the supervisor is apt to be hurled down from a shaky pedestal with some force. The capacity of both to bear this loss of admiration as a normal aspect of learning will enable the student to grow and move on to the next phase.

EXAMPLE: Ms. J. was being supervised by Dr. R., whom she deeply admired and held in some awe. She was a dedicated student whose prior training was scanty and she approached the present situation eagerly. She read everything Dr. R. suggested (especially his own publications), took copious notes of the supervision hour, and became an ardent devotee of his well-known method for treating certain kinds of borderline patients. It was impossible not to notice that she even emulated his verbal habits and his hand gestures.

Dr. R., who was a wise and experienced supervisor, tolerated this adoration and was braced for the inevitable day when he would fall from grace. Ms. J. reported with great distress that her patient had made a major suicide attempt, was hospitalized, and that the inpatient doctor had chided her for inadequate use of psychotropic medication with this patient. Ms. J. clearly felt terrible and blamed a psychopharmacological consultation for all her patient's difficulties, which she reported with some coldness and defiance in the supervision. Dr. R. patiently tolerated the anger while helping her focus on the fearful impotence that she felt with her patient. Eventually, as Ms. J. felt less terror for the patient and for herself, she regained her equilibrium and continued the work with Dr. R. with a much deeper appreciation of his support and tutelage.

Identification

In the process of identification, one person uses the other as an auxiliary ego. For example, a clinician may be repelled by a patient whose plight makes him anxious. In presenting this situation in supervision, the supervisor discusses the patient's pain and the dilemma this causes the helpers with empathy and respect for both. The clinician can appreciate the supervisor's mellowing attitude, and recall it consciously to mind during the hour with the patient. It is not unusual at this stage for the trainee to say such things as "I felt like getting up and leaving, but then I thought, what would you (my supervisor) say to this patient, and I didn't feel at such a loss." Thus the trainee moves from "slave" to "apostle" at this stage, and begins to feel much more dedicated to the clinical stance of the supervisor, while maintaining some capacity for thinking autonomously and using his own language and judgment.

The supervisor's role at this stage is to offer examples from his own practice with some clear discussions of the pros and cons of any situation, and to continue to encourage the trainee to experiment a bit. The supervisor must be willing to encourage some levels of safe-enough risk-taking, and freely to admit to ignorance when confronted with some puzzling questions. Essentially, he is stepping away from any idealizable position, and building expectations for the tolerance of ambiguity.

EXAMPLE: To continue from the prior example, Ms. J. told her supervisor that next time her patient reported suicidal ideation during the hour she was able to take a deep breath, think of Dr. R. and hear him say "You want me to know how impotent you feel." She was able to discuss

128

this helplessness with the patient and for a time, at least, was able to feel competent and useful to her patient.

Integration

One of the more exciting and more difficult tasks that confronts the trainee in this stage is integrating several identifications and evolving an autonomous clinical self. This is enabled by the fact that trainees have a number of supervisors, each of whom brings some idiosyncratic aspects to the work. Each supervisor sees the case differently, and can tell you why. Each supervisor speaks to patients differently, and has a rationale for doing so. Finally, each supervisor deals differently with supervision, and when pressed should be able to explain why. Since these methods have all proven to have some merit and some limitations, the trainee is then free to pick and choose those aspects of each that are consistent with his own personality, stage of life, and treatment preferences.

Supervisors encourage this process by their willingness to discuss the implied assumptions by which they operate and maintain a strong and clearly defined stance, yet respect the wide range of curative and training styles that permeate the field. Usually the student is only asked to comply for the duration of supervision. In the example above, Dr. R. was clear about his rationale for treatment, and encouraged Ms. J. to discuss the case more fully and openly with the consultant at the hospital. He also encouraged her to familiarize herself with more aspects of psychopharmacology and to use an informed and independent judgment about her cases in the future.

End phase supervision

Consistent with the position that supervision replicates and models treatment, the evaluation and termination of the work constitutes the end phase and requires the same careful attention as all other phases.

Evaluation

In an optimal supervision, critcism of the work has been continuous and constructive, and the final evaluation should hold no surprises for anyone. Measured against the contracted baseline, the evaluation can be more objective. Since the work consists of the development of the clinician as viewed in all aspects of the case at hand, the personal and the clinical competence of the trainee has been the subject of the work throughout. The supervisory relationship provides another major boundary for examining the student's clinical competence by allowing the supervisor to ask such questions as: How has the student used the supervision? What is the quality of our relationship? How open has he been to new learning and to self-exposure? How psychological-minded? What is his capacity for empathy? For decisiveness? These questions need constant reassessment throughout any careful training program; the input of the supervisors is obviously a major yardstick for evaluating both the student and the training program. It provides an opportunity to congratulate the trainee expressly on his competence, and to express appreciation for the work done. It is also a time for the supervisor to make clear recommendations for future directions of training. It is well to remember, however, that often this is a sensitive time for the student, especially if the work had its troublesome aspects. The collaboration of the trainee with the supervisor in the writing of the supervisory evaluation is crucial at these times. One approach is to ask the student to write the first draft of the evaluation, which will then be amended by the supervisor. This process can continue until both are satisfied with the fairness of the report, which they then both sign and turn in to the director of training. This method is recommended for a variety of reasons. To allow for future growth, the evaluation must be done in such a way that the trainee feels respected and heard. To the extent that the student's own metaphors and words are used, he can feel more like an active learner. The supervisor must also feel free to exercise judgment and authority. Both voices and positions must be clearly articulated; both must continue a learning collaboration that extends into the final evaluation report. The standards of quality set by the supervisor evolve into a shared commitment to quality control for their mutual profession.

The evaluation process needs to be worked through in order for termination to occur. Both parties must have a chance to express appreciation and affection. Both must have the opportunity and courage to discuss the disappointments, and to forgive that which was not always easy to forgive. It is important to remember that today's supervisory dyad is part of tomorrow's collegial group, and great efforts must be made to enchance the opportunity for continued professional regard and contact. It is also to be hoped that the graduating clinicians will be encouraged to become supervisors themselves, and carry the best of their supervisory experiences into the work with their future trainees.

A supervisory evaluation form

Supervisory evaluation forms range from attempts to quantify a student's specific strengths and liabilities, to more general requests about overall progress. The following is an example: an evaluation that attends to the supervisory dyad's relationship to the student's skills, and to the supervisor's recommendations for the student's continuing development. It is specifically designed for supervisors of psychotherapy, and does not include evaluation of other clinical skills, such as psychopharmacologic/psychometric comprehension and usage.

Dear Supervisor,

Twice a year, in January and in June, we will need an evaluation of your supervision with _____. Please give us your clear opinion of his clinical competence, paying special attention to the following, while adding whatever else you may see fit:

131

1. The trainee's capacity to form a warm and respectful alliance with the patient, and with you.
2. His capacity to be psychologically minded; to be empathic; to tolerate ambiguity; to move decisively when necessary; to separate self from patient.
3. What is the trainee's level of theoretical sophistication? How invested is he in studying theory, in examining and organizing and abstracting data? In applying theory to the case at hand?
4. Is the student ethical? Can he work within the administrative constraints of an organization? Is he systematic and careful about the frame issues, such as fees, record-keeping, punctuality, and coverage?
5. How does the trainee relate to you? Is he serious? Fun to be with? Open-minded and receptive? Argumentative and challenging? Are there some kinds of patients you would hesitate to refer to this trainee at this stage of clinical development?
6. What are your recommendations for the next period of training? What do you judge to be requirements for arriving at an adequate level of professional competence? How aware is the trainee of his strengths and deficits, and how accepting of recommendations for future training?

Please keep in mind that we rely heavily on your input to reshape our training program. We take your evaluations seriously; so do our trainees in planning their future work.

Thank you for this contribution.

_____/Signed by Director of Training

Summary

This chapter describes the course of a supervision in concrete and specific terms. While any number of variations may be added to meet the preferences and needs of a particular training system, they are usually amended versions of the supervisory structure as delineated here.

Reference

1. Reik, T. *Listening with the Third Ear.* New York: Grove Press, 1948.

9

A Model
Program for
Psychotherapy
Supervisors

Fundamental to any program of clinical supervision is an attitude of open-minded collegiality in the faculty and in the administration of the training institution. Such an attitude bespeaks high levels of trust and respect that are apparent in a willingness to expose one's work to colleagues in the same way as the system expects the trainees to expose their work to the faculty. This kind of directness generates a healthy learning atmosphere in which supervisors take pride in demonstrating their special areas of competence, seek consultation freely from one another, and examine training failures in a responsible and self-reflective way.

While this utopian situation is rare, there are ways of moving even the most entrenched system in this direction. Increased attentiveness to and dialogue with the supervisors will go a long way toward generating energy for change. It is past time for supervision to move from a quiet to a more vocal and conscious profession. To this end, the following organizational plan is proposed. It has been tried and found to be effective in a few settings. While obviously each system will need to tailor the process to make it appropriate to its own idiosyncratic realities, in the main it should apply to the great majority of training programs in the United States.

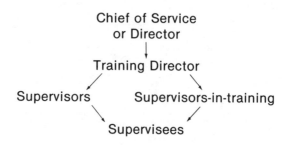

Chief of Service
or Director

Training Director

Supervisors   Supervisors-in-training

Supervisees

The executive director of the program

The philosophy of the training program is primarily generated and represented by the executive director of the program (sometimes known as the Chief of Service). This person may be the chief of the department of psychiatry or psychology, or any clearly designated head of the training and treatment system. This is the person who decides on the relative value assigned to training and to service. His decisions determine the budget and thus the hiring practices for faculty. More important, the clinical and training biases of this person will have a major impact on the entire supervisory work, as will such personal attitudes as self-confidence, clinical enthusiasm, and an ability to admit to error and vulnerability. So will his career emphasis; is the executive director a clinician primarily? A supervisor? An administrator? A researcher? If the director is not a clinician or supervisor primarily, how much is he able to delegate these aspects of training to someone who is passionately dedicated to the teaching and learning of psychotherapy? This becomes a major concern in a climate of diminished funding for training. Indeed, the survival of most of the training programs in the country speaks to the vision and objectivity of the majority of the directors of clinical systems. Many have felt the need to improvise and reconsider old habits of functioning even at the risk of alienating some of their professional colleagues. Often, they have forged partnerships with previously unallied professional resources to do so, and have been forced to make some hard choices relative to cost accountability and deployment of resources in their existing structures.

Some of these compromises have disequilibrated old aspects of the status quo, for better and for worse. For example, in many hospital-based programs there exists a quid-pro-quo system, in which part-time members of the department receive a hospital appointment in exchange for being available to supervise for three or four hours a week. Originally this was a gentleman's agreement in which a potential supervisor might or might not make himself available, and the system might or might not choose him as a supervisor. The executive director had funds to hire other supervisors when needed, and the loose collaboration continued. With diminished financial resources for training, directors need to use the part-time staff as supervisors, which creates a situation in which old and loyal compatriots in the department may be offended. The commitment to psychotherapy training must be very strong in the director's list of priorities to invite this kind of delicate juggling of resources. Furthermore, the director must be able and willing to withstand the press of the demands for service in order to release the trainees for supervision. The supervisory hour must be retained for that purpose alone, and space and other resources must be provided.

Most importantly, the departmental head can convey a sense of dignity and status to the supervisors by hiring a director of training who is valued in the department and perceived as a major figure in policy setting for the entire clinical program.

The director of training

In addition to overseeing student training, this person is responsible for the training and maintenance of supervisors, and the retention of some of the retiring members of the training faculty for their wisdom and counsel. For the director of training to accomplish these goals he must enjoy the confidence of the executive director and be given a clear mandate to balance training and service needs in a way that is acceptable to and understood by all parties in the training program.

The training of clinicians

Since the director is responsible for a balanced and well-rounded training experience, it is crucial that he have a part in arranging the match between supervisor and student. The trainee needs an opportunity to work with both male and female supervisors at all levels of age and experience. In addition, the supervisors should represent a broad spectrum of clinical theory and application.

On the other hand, the issue of personal attraction is a serious one; the chance of supervision succeeding is related to the sense of personal liking to some extent. Probably the ideal situation is one in which there is some balance of assignment of supervisors, and some free choice. The latter of course depends on the attraction being mutual; the trainee always runs the risk of choosing a supervisor who may not necessarily have chosen the student, and vice versa. However, given everybody's good will, this can usually be made to work in the student's interest.

In case of intractable impasse, the director needs to inform the supervisor and the supervisee of their options. A clearly outlined set of procedures for seeking consultation, and an atmosphere that encourages the use of consultation as a positive step becomes a clear message of back-up support for the two parties, and underscores the seriousness of the enterprise. It is advisable for the director of training first to meet with both parties to the impasse, separately and together; if this does not suffice, then he might refer them to a senior supervisory consultant designated in the system, perhaps on a rotating basis. This person serves both as an impartial consultant and as an ombudsman in the system, while also being in a position to offer data first-hand should further administrative action be needed.

Close record-keeping of impasse situations will help in a number of ways; (a) by providing opportunities for research into the supervisory process, (b) by signaling recurring kinds of problems in the department that may be related to peculiarities in the system; (c) by generating excellent guidelines for positive resolution of impasse based on previous experience of success.

The training and maintenance of supervisors

For junior members who are about to begin supervision there needs to be a period of formal training in how to supervise; this is best done in a biweekly seminar where the new supervisor presents the supervision hour for the entire group's advice and counsel. More experienced supervisors should regularly be invited to participate. This is often their only formal look at the process and theory of supervision, and it can revitalize what is threatening to become a burdensome rote chore. Frequently it is the first time they have discussed their supervisory methods with colleagues, and most supervisors welcome the opportunity.

This kind of seminar must be protected from deflecting the anxiety of disclosure of the supervisors by focusing on the troublesome student only. Thus the seminar leader needs to steer the focus to the supervisor's consciousness of self and on increasing the supervisor's options for functioning in the hour with the student.

One way to utilize this seminar is to launch some research on the supervisory process, which then serves to focus the members on theory as well as practice, and to increase the data base for future training of supervisors.

The director of training must be attentive to the supervisors' preferences and needs in the kinds of students assigned and to the normal need for expressed appreciation for the work they do. In particular, if a supervisor has struggled with an especially difficult situation one year, a more promising student should be assigned when possible. Also, that supervisor should be invited to discuss the troublesome experience in depth so that all parties of the training system can take advantage of the wisdom he acquired.

Retention of senior or retiring supervisors

The quality of a community is related to the acknowledgment of dignity in its senior citizens. They are in a position to contribute immeasurably to the culture by sharing their accumulated wisdom and by offering constructive criticism of the training process. The channel for this exchange remains to be developed in most training institutions. It would be of great value to interview senior supervisors about their work; to generate videotapes or other "live" recordings of their supervision; to include them in the training of supervisors as teachers or consultants to the seminar; to call upon them to resolve supervisory impasse, etc.

When should training of supervisors begin, and how?

The profession of supervision is far too important and complex to be haphazardly patched onto a general clinical practice. A logical progression of recruitment, training, mentoring, and continuing education is needed for the development of a full professional sub-specialty. In the same way that not every clinician is suited or inclined to be an analyst, an administrator, or a psychopharmacologist, not everyone wants to or can supervise.

Taken as a sub-specialty, the selection and training track for supervisors can resemble that of any other in the field. For example, a chief residency in supervision can be established under the aegis of the director of training.

A similar position can be created in their training programs. This person would work with senior supervisors to organize the supervision seminar for students in their last year of training, work with the director of training to collate the data from supervisory evaluations, conduct research on supervision, track the training of junior trainees, help to plan supervisory assignments, and help to identify and recruit promising members of the supervisory seminar to continue on as novice supervisors in the department.

More experienced supervisors would play a major role in the program by being assigned as mentors to the novice supervisors. They can participate in teaching and learning supervision through the seminar described above, and in more informal ways. Their contribution would be much more visible in the department, and would, it is hoped, encourage additions to the literature on supervision.

The Trainees

In a system where the trainers are openly acknowledged and valued, the trainees are also held in high esteem. Given the painful realities of psychotherapy training, any process that makes a major and positive impact on the self-esteem of the clinicians-in-training is golden. The effects of such a benign loop permeate the system, from the patient, through to the administration, and to the perception and appreciation of the clinical profession by the culture at large.

Finally, supervisors of psychotherapy would be well served by the formation of a validating natural body, an Association of Psychotherapy Supervisors. Since psychotherapy cuts across professional disciplines, such an organization would be a multidisciplinary organ for encouraging dialogue, research, collegiality, and continuing education. Most importantly, supervision could take its rightful place as a clinical speciality, and its quiet practitioners would be awarded the dignity that is their due.

Bibliography

Aarons, Z. A. 1974. The application of psychoanalysis to psychiatric training, *Int. J. Psychiatry*, 3 (2), 178–203.

Adamson, J., Prosen, H., & Bebchuk W. 1968. Training in formal psycho–therapy in the psychiatric residency program. *Can. Psychiatr. Assoc. J.*, 13 (5), 445–454.

Alonso, A., & Rutan, J. 1978. Cross-sex supervision for cross-sex therapy. *Am. J. Psychiatry*, 135 (8), 928–931.

Allen, D. W., Houston, M., & McCarley, Jr., T. H. 1958. Resistances to learning. *J. Med. Educ.*, 33, 373–379.

Anderson, B., Pine, I., & Mee-Lee, D. 1972. Resident training in cotherapy groups. *Int. J. Group Psychother.*, 22, 192–198.

Argyle, M. 1972. *The social psychology of work.* Harmondsworth, Eng.: Penguin Books.

Arsenian, J. 1968. Life cycle factors in mental illness. *Mental Hygiene*, 52, 1.

Austin, L. 1952. Basic principles of supervision. *Social Casework*, 33, 416.

Bachrach, H., Luborsky, L., & Mechanick, P. 1974. The correspondence between judgments of empathy from brief samples of psychotherapy, supervisors' judgments and sensitivity tests. *Brit. J. Med. Psychol*, 47, 337–340.

Bales, R. F. 1951. Interaction process analysis. Cambridge, MA.: Addison-Wesley Press, Inc.

Balint, A. 1937. The part played by the analyst's personality in the handling of the transference: Report of the first Four Countries Conference. *Int. J. Psychoanal.*, 18, 60–61.

Balsam, A., & Garber, N. 1970. Characteristics of psychotherapy supervision. *J. Med. Educ.*, 45, 788–797.

Baltes, P. B. 1968. Longitudinal and cross-section sequences in the study of age and generation effects. *Hum. Dev.*, II, 3, 145–171.

Baltes, P. B., & Willis, S. L. 1977. Toward psychological theories of aging and development. In J. E. Birren & K. W. Schaie (Eds.), *Handbook on psychology of aging*. New York: Reinhold-Von Nostrand.

Barron, F. 1963. Personal soundness in university graduate students. In *Creativity and psychological health*. Princeton, NJ: D. Van Nostrand Co.

Bateson, G., Jackson, D. D., Haley, J., & Weakland, J. 1956. Toward a theory of schizophrenia. *Behavioral Science*, 1, 251–264.

Berger, D., & Freebury, D. 1973. The acquisition of psychotherapy skills: A learning model and some guidelines for instructors. *Can. Psychiatr. Assoc. J.*, 18, 467–471.

Bibring, E. *et al.* 1937. Discussion on control analysis. *Int. J. Psychol-Anal.*, 18, 369.

Birren, J. 1964. *The psychology of aging*. Englewood Cliffs, NJ: Prentice-Hall.

Birren, J. E., & Schaie, K. W. (Eds.). 1977. *Handbook of the psychology of aging*. New York: Van Nostrand.

Bischoff, L. J. 1976. *Adult Psychology* (2nd ed). New York: Harper & Row.

Blaxell, M., & Reagan, B. 1976. *Women and the workplace*. Chicago: University of Chicago Press.

Bocknek, G. 1976. A developmental approach to counseling adults. *J. Couns. Psychol.*, 6(1) 37–40.

Book, H. 1973. On maybe becoming a psychotherapist, perhaps. *Can. Psychiatr. Assoc. J.*, 18, 487–492.

Borges, J. L. 1966. *Other Acquisitions, 1937–1952*. NY: Washington Square Press, Inc., pp. 1–4.

Boris, H. 1976. On hope: Its nature in psychotherapy. *Int. J. Psychoanal.*, 3, 139–150.

Borus, J. F. & Groves, J. E. 1982. Training Supervision as a Separate Faculty Role. *Am. J. Psychiatry*, 139, pp. 1339–1342.

Botwinick, J. 1967. *Cognitive processes in maturity and old age*. New York: Springer.

Brady, J. P. 1967. Psychotherapy, learning theory, and insight. *Arch. Gen. Psychiatry*, **16**, 304–311.

Bray, D. W. 1964. The management progress study. *The American Psychologist*, **19**(6), 419–420. (Reprint.)

Brenner, C. 1982. *The mind in conflict*. NY: International University Press, Inc.

Brim, O.G. 1974. The sense of personal control over one's live. *82nd Annual Convention of the APA, New Orleans.*

Broverman, I., *et al.* 1970. Sex role stereotypes and clinical judgments of mental health. *J. Consult and Clinical Psychol.*, **34**, 1–7.

Bucher, R., Stelling, J., & Dommermuth, P. 1969. Implications of prior socialization for residency programs in psychiatry. *Arch. Gen. Psychiatry*, **20**, 395–402.

Buckley, W. 1967. *Sociology and modern systems theory*. Englewood Cliffs, NJ: Prentice-Hall.

Buie, D., & Adler, G. 1973. The uses of confrontation in the psychotherapy of borderline cases. In G. Adler, & P. Myerson (Eds.), *Confrontation in Psychotherapy*. New York: Science House.

Buhler, C. 1930. *The course of human life*. New York: John Day Co.

Burgoyne, R., Kline, F., Goin, M., Woods, S., & Peck, S. 1978. Observed psychotherapy—what the patients say about it. *J. Psychiatr. Educ.*, **2**, 83–92.

Bury, J., Labrie, J., & Pomerleau, G. 1973. L'enseignement de l'approche psychodynamique en première année de residence en psychiatrie. *L'Union Medicale du Canada*, **102**(3), 620–623.

Carlson, D. (Ed.). 1970. *Generation in the middle*. Chicago: Blue Cross Association.

Cervantes, M. de., *Don Quixote*, 1957. Chap. 9. p. 1605, trans. by W. Starkey, London: MacMillan, p. 109.

Char, W. 1971. The foreign resident: An ambivalently valued object. *Psychiatry*, **34**, 234–238.

Chessick, R. D. 1969. *How psychotherapy heals*. New York: Science Hours.

Chessick, R. D. 1971. How the resident and the supervisor disappoint each other. *Am. J. Psychother.* **25**, 272–283.

Chessick, R. D. 1971. Why psychotherapists fail. NY: Science Hours.

Chirviboga, D., & Lowenthal, M. 1974. Personality: Happiness is complexity in youth, simplicity in age. (Newsline) *Psychology Today*, Aug., pp. 34–35.

Chodoff, P. 1972. Supervision of psychotherapy with videotape: Pros and cons. *Am. J. Psychiatry*, **128**(7), 319–823.

Clemence, E. 1965. The dynamic use of ego psychiatry in casework education. *Smith College Studies in Social Work*, XXXV, 3.

Clausen, J. 1972. The life course of individuals. *Aging and Society, 3; The sociology of age stratification.* New York: The Russell Sage Foundation.

Cohen, R. S., & De Betz, B. 1977. Responsive supervision of the psychiatric resident and clinical psychology intern. *Am. J. Psychoanal.,* **37,** 51–64.

DeBeauvoir, S. 1973. *The coming of age.* New York: Warner Paperback.

Deikman, A. J. 1971. Bimodal consciousness. *Arch. Gen. Psychiatry,* **25,** 481–489.

Dellis, N., & Stone, H. 1960. *The training of psychotherapists.* Baton Rouge, LA; Louisiana State University Press.

DeRosis, H. Supervision of the first year psychiatric resident. *Psychiatr. Quart.* Part I–44, 1970, 3, 435–442; Part II –215, 1971, 1, 134–141; Parts III & IV –45, 1971, 2, 289–298; Parts V & VI –45, 1971, 3, 423–439; Parts VII & VIII –45, 1971, 4, 559–573; Part IX –46, 1972, 2, 284–303; Part XI –47, 1973, 3, 442–457.

Deutsch, H. 1953. Occult processes occurring during psychoanalysis. In G. Devereaux (Ed.), *Psychoanalysis and the occult.* New York: International Universities Press.

DeVito, R., Denshaw, D., & Delisi, S. 1969. Peer supervision among psychiatric residents. *Brit. J. Med. Educ.,* **3,** 62–65.

D'Zmura, T. 1964. The function of individual supervision. *Int. Psychiatr. Clin.* **1,** 381.

Ebaugh, F. 1950–51. Graduate teaching of psychiatry through individual supervision. *Am. J. Psychiatry,* **107,** 274–278.

Einstein, A. 1956. *Letters to Maurice Solvine.* Paris: Gauttier-Vietars.

Ekstein, R., & Wallerstein, R. S. 1963. *The teaching and learning of psychotherapy.* New York: Basic Books.

Elder, G. H., Jr. 1975. Age differentiation and the life course. *Annual Review of Sociology,* **I,** pp. 165–190.

Elmore, J. L. 1970. Adaptation to aging. *The Gerontologist,* **10,** 50–53.

Emeh, M. 1955. The social context of supervision. *Int. J. Psychoanal.,* **36,** 298.

Erikson, E. 1950. *Childhood and society.* New York: W. W. Norton Co., Inc.

Erikson, E. 1959. Identity and the life cycle: Selected papers. *Psychological Issues.* (Monograph No. 1).

Erikson, E. 1964. Insight and responsibility. New York: W. W. Norton Co., Inc.

Erikson, E. 1968. Identity, youth and crisis. New York: W. W. Norton Co., Inc.

Erikson, E. 1978. Adulthood. New York: W. W. Norton Co., Inc.

Fix, A. J., & Hoffke, E. A. 1975. Relationship between psychotherapy skills and level of training in a psychiatric residency program. *Soc. Sci. Med.*, 9, 489–491.

Fleming, H., & Benedek, T. 1966. *Psychoanalytic supervision.* New York: Grune & Stratton.

Fontaine, P. 1975. Equipé et formation au centre université de guidance infantile à volume (Bruxelles). *Acta Psychiatr. Belg.*, 75, 899–904.

Fozard, J. L., & Popkin, S. J. 1978. Optimizing adult development: Ends and means of an applied psychology of aging. *Am. Psychologist*, 33(11), 975–990.

Frank, J. 1974. *Persuasion and healing* (Rev. ed.). New York: Schocken Books.

Freud, A. 1958. On adolescence. *Psychoanalytic study of the child (13). New York: International Universities Press.*

Freud, S. Letter to Fleiss, March 10, 1898—Freud, 1950a, Letter 84, The *Origins of Psychoanalysis*, Standard Ed., I.

Freud, S. 1901. The psychopathology of everyday life, Standard Edition, VI.

Freud, S. 1910. The future prospects of psychoanalytic therapy, Standard Edition, 11, 141.

Freud, S. 1917. Introductory lectures on psychoanalysis. Lecture XVIII—Fixation to Traumas—the Unconscious, Standard edition, III, 278.

Freud, S. (1912) 1959. The dynamics of the transference. In E. Jones (Ed.) *Collected papers.* New York: Basic Books.

Frey, L., & Dubois, E. 1972. Andragogy and social work supervision. Unpublished manuscript.

Frijling-Schreuder, E. 1970. On individual supervision. *Int. J. Psychoanal.*, 52, 84–89.

Gaskill, H., & Norton, J. 1968. Observations on psychiatric residency training. *Arch. Gen. Psychiatry*, 18, 7–15.

Gilligan, C. 1982. *In A Different Voice.* Cambridge, Harvard University Press.

Giovacchini, P. 1972. Tactics and techniques in psychoanalytic therapy. New York: Science House, (Ed.).

Gladfelter, J. W. 1970. Videotape supervision of co-therapists on videotape techniques. In M. Berger (Ed.), *Psychiatric training and treatment.* New York: Bruner-Mazel.

Glenn, N. D. 1974. Aging and conservatism. *The Annals of the American Academy.* pp. 176–186. (Sept.)

Glenn, N. D. 1975. Psychological well-being in the postparental stage:

Some evidence from national surveys. *J. Marriage and the Family.* pp. 105–110. (February).

Goin, M., & Kline, F. 1976. Countertransference: A neglected subject in clinical supervision. *Am. J. Psychiatry,* **133**(1), 141–144.

Gould, R. 1970. Preventive psychiatry and the field theory of reality. *J. Am. Psychoanal. Assoc.,* **18**, 2.

Gould, R. 1972. The phases of adult life: A study in developmental psychology. *Am. J. Psychiatry,* **129**, 521–531.

Gould, R. 1975. Adult life stages: Growth toward self tolerance. *Psychology Today,* 8, 9.

Gould, R. 1978. *Transformations.* New York: Simon & Schuster.

Greben, S., Markson, E., and Sadavoy, J. 1973. Resident and supervisor: An examination of their relationship. *Can. Psychiatr. Assoc. J.,* **18**, 473–478.

Greenson, R., & Wexler, M. 1969. The non-transference relationship in the psychoanalytic situation. *Int. J. Psychoanal.,* **50** (270, 27–39.

Greenson, R. 1972. *The technique and practice of psychoanalysis.* New York: International Universities Press.

Greer, G. 1970. *The female eunuch.* New York: McGraw-Hill.

Grinker, R. R. 1962. Mentally healthy young males (homoclites). Achievement-related conflicts in women. *J. Soc. Issues,* **28**(2), 157–174.

Grotjohn, M. 1955. Problems and techniques of supervision. *Int. J. Psychoanal.,* **36**, 298.

Grotjohn, M. 1949. The role of identification in psychiatric and psychoanalytic training." *Psychiatry,* **12**, 141.

Haan, N. 1964. The relationship of ego functioning and intelligence to social status and social mobility. *J. Abnorm. and Social Psychol.,* **69**(8), 354–405.

Halleck, S., & Woods, S. 1962. Emotional problems of psychiatric residents. *Psychiatry,* **25**, 339.

Hamburg, D. A., Coelho, G., & Adams, J. E. (Eds.). 1974. *Coping and adaptation.* New York: Basic Books.

Hamburg, D. A., & Adams, J. E. 1967. A perspective on coping behavior. *Arch. Gen. Psychiatry,* **17**, 277–284.

Hamilton, J. 1971. Some aspects of learning, supervision and identity formation in the psychiatric residency. *Psychiatr. Quart.,* **45**(3), 410–422.

Hawthorne, L. 1975. Games supervisors play. *Social Work,* **20**, 179–183.

Hess, A. (Ed.). 1980. *Psychotherapy supervision: Theory, research, and practice.* New York: John Wiley & Sons.

Hester, L., Weitz, L., Roback, H., *et al.* 1976. The supervisor/supervisee relationship in psychotherapy training from the perspective of interpersonal attraction. *Compr. Psychiatry*, 17, (5), pp. 671–681.

Holland, J. L. 1966. The psychology of vocational choice—A theory of personality types and model environments. Waltham, MA: Blaisdell Press.

Horner, M. 1972. Toward an understanding of achievement-related conflicts in women. *J. Soc. Issues*, 28(2), 157–174.

Jacobs, B., & Slakler, E. 1974. Some considerations of after-care: Problems of therapy, training, and preceptoring. *Int. J. Psychoanal. Psychother.*, 3, 116–123.

Johnson, P. 1971. *The middle years.* Fortress Press.

Jones, E. 1951. The god complex. In *Essays in applied psychoanalysis.* London: Hogarth Press, (II:244).

Jourard, S. 1964. *The transparent self.* Princeton, N.J.: Van Nostrand.

Jung, C. 1933. The stages of life. Modern man in search of a soul. In W. S. Dell, & C. Baynes (Trans.), London and New York; J. Campbell (Ed.), *The Portable Jung.* 1971, translation by R.F.C. Hull, 1971.

Kadushin, A. 1968. Games people play in supervision. *Social Work*, 13, 23–32.

Kadushin, A. 1976. *Supervision in social work.* N.Y.: Columbia University Press.

Kagan, J., & Moss, H. 1962. *From birth to maturity.* N.Y.: John Wiley & Sons.

Kahn, E. M. 1979. The parallel process in social work treatment and supervision. *Social Casework*, 60(9), 500–528.

Kasius, C. (Ed.). 1962. *Social casework in the fifties.* N.Y.: Fam. Serv. Assoc. of America.

Kaslow, F., & Associates. 1978. *Supervision, consultation, and staff training in the helping professions.* San Francisco, CA: Jossey-Bass, Inc.

Kastenbaum, R. 1965. Theories of human aging; the search for a conceptual framework. J. Social Issues, (Oct.), pp. 13–36.

Kelley, E. L. 1955. Consistency of the adult personality. *Am. Psychol.*, 10, 659–681.

Kernberg, O. 1975. *Borderline Conditions and Pathological Narcissism.* N.Y.: Jason Aronson, Inc.

Kleemeir, R. W. 1959. Behavior and the organization of the bodily and the external environment. In J. E. Birren (Ed.), *Handbook of aging and the individual.* Chicago: University of Chicago Press.

153

Klein, M. (1932). 1975. The psychoanalysis of children. In *The writings of Melanie Klein.* London: Hogarth Press.

Knoff, W., Oken, D., & Prevost, J. 1976. Meeting training needs of foreign psychiatric residence in state hospitals. *Hosp. Commun. Psychiatry,* **27,** (1), 35–37.

Knowles, M. S. 1970. The modern practice of adult education: Andragogy vs. pedagogy. N.Y.: Association Press.

Kohut, H. 1977. *The restoration of the self.* N.Y.: International Universities Press.

Kraft-Goin, M., Kaline, F. 1976. Countertransference—a neglected subject in supervision. *Am. J. Psychiatry,* **133,** 1.

Kritzer, H., & Langsley, D. 1967. Training for emergency psychiatric services. *J. Med. Educ.,* **42,** 1111–1115.

Kubie, L. 1958. Research into the process of supervision in psychoanalysis. *Psychoanal. Quart.,* **7,** 226–236.

Kuhlen, R. G. 1963. Age and Intelligence: The significance of cultural change in longitudinal vs. cross-sectional findings. *Vita Humana,* **6,** 113–124.

Lakovics, M. 1976. Some problems in learning to do good psychotherapy. *Am. J. Psychiatry,* **133**(7), 834–837.

Lamberd, W., Adamson, J., & Burdick, J. 1972. A study of self-image experience in student psychotherapists.*J. Nerv. Ment. Dis.,* **155**(3), 184–191.

Langs, R. 1976. *The bipersonal field.* New York: Jason Aronson.

Langs, R. 1978. *The listening process.* N.Y.: Jason Aronson.

Langs, R. 1979. *The supervisory experience.* N.Y.: Jason Aronson.

Lazerson, A. 1972. The learning alliance and its relation to psychiatric teaching. *Psychiatry Med.,* **3,** 81–91.

Lerner, H. 1974. Early origins of envy and devaluation of women: Implications for sex role stereotypes. *Bull. Menninger Clin,* **38,** 538–553.

LeShan, E. 1973. *The wonderful crisis of middle age.* N.Y.: David McKay, Ed.

Levene, H., Breger, L., & Patterson, V. A training and research program in brief psychotherapy. *Am. J. Psychother.*

Levinson, D. J., Darrow, C. M., Klein, E. B., Levinson, M. H., & McKee, B. 1974. The psychosocial development of man in early adulthood and the mid-life transition. To appear in D. F. Ricks, A. Thomas, & M. Roff (Eds.), *Life history research in psychopathology 3.* Minn.: University of Minnesota Press.

Levinson, D. J. 1978. *The seasons of a man's life.* N.Y.: Alfred Knopf, Inc.

Lewis, J. 1974. Practicum in attention to affect: A course for beginning psychotherapists. *Psychiatry, 37*, 109–113.

Lewis, J. M. 1978. *To be a therapist: The teaching and learning of empathy.* N.Y.: Brunner/Mazel.

Lewis, M., & Colletti, R. 1973. Child psychiatry teaching in pediatric training: The use of a study group. *Pediatrics, 52*(5), 743–745.

Lementani, A. 1974. The training analyst and the difficulties in the training psychoanalytic situation. *Int. J. Psychoanal.*, pp. 55–71.

Little, W., Fowler, H. W., & Coulson, J. 1959. *The shorter Oxford english dictionary,* C. T. Onions, Ed. Oxford: The Clarendon Press.

Loewinger, R., & Wessler, R. 1970. *Measuring ego development:* San Francisco: Jossey-Bass.

Lowenthal, M. F. 1971. Intentionality: Toward a framework for the study of adaptation in adulthood. *Aging Hum. Dev., 2*, 79–95.

Lowenthal, M. F., Thurnber, M., & Chiriboga, D. 1976. *Four stages of life.* San Francisco, CA: Jossey-Bass, Inc.

Lower, R. 1972. Countertransference resistances in the supervisory situation. *Am. J. Psychiatry, 129* (2), 156–169.

Maddon, G. L. 1968. Persistance of lifestyle among the elderly. In B. Neugarten (Ed.), *Middle age and aging.* Chicago: University of Chicago Press.

Maccoby, E. M., & Jacklin, G. N. 1974. *The psychology of sex differences.* CA: Stanford University Press.

Mahler, M. S. 1965. In the significance of the normal-individuation phase: With reference to research in symbiotic child psychosis. In M. Schur (Ed.), *Drives, affects, behavior,* 2. N.Y.: International Universities Press.

Mahler, M. S. 1961. On human symbiosis and vicissitudes of individuation. In *Infantile Psychosis.* N.Y.: International Universities Press.

Mahler, M. S. 1971. *Presentations and publications of Margaret Mahler,* R. C. Proll (Ed.). New York: International Universities Press.

Marmor, J. 1953. The feeling of superiority; an occupational hazard in the practice of psychotherapy. *Am. J. Psychother.*

Marmor, J. 1979. Psychoanalytic training. Arch. Gen. Psychiatr., 36, (April), pp. 486–492.

Maslow, A. 1968. *Toward a psychology of being.* New York: Van Nostrand Co.

McClelland, D. 1961. *The achieving society.* N.Y.: Van Nostrand Co.

McClelland, D. 1975. *Power: The inner experience.* N.Y.: Irvington Publishers.

Mehlman, R. 1974. Becoming and being a psychotherapist: The problem of narcissism. *Int. J. Psychiatry*, **3**, 125–141.

Millett, A., & Burstein, A. 1969. Professional development in psychiatric residents. *Arch. Gen. Psychiatry*, **20**, 385–394.

Miller, J. 1976. *Toward a new psychology of women*, Boston, MA: Beacon Press.

Millet, K. 1970. *Sexual politics*. N.Y.: Doubleday.

Morrison, A., Shore, M., & Grobman, J. 1973. On the stresses of community psychiatry and helping residents to survive them. *Am. J. Psychiatry*, **130**(11), 1237–1241.

Mosher, F., & Purpel, D. 1972. *Supervision: The reluctant profession.* Boston, MA: Houghton Mifflin, Co.

Murdaugh, J. 1974. Student supervision. *Social Work*, March, **19**(2), 131.

Muslin, H. Burstein, A., Gedo, J., & Sadow, L. 1967. Research on the supervisory process. *Arch. Gen. Psychiatry*, **16**, 427–531.

Nadelson, C., & Notman, M. 1977. Psychotherapy supervision. The problem of conflicting values. *Am. J. Psychotherapy*, **31**(2), 275–283.

Nesselroade, J. R., & Reese, H. W. (Eds.). 1973. Life span developmental psychology. In *Methodological issues.* N.Y.: Academic Press, Inc.

Neugarten, B. L. The awareness of middle ages. In *Middle Age*.

Neugarten, B. L. 1977. Personality and aging. In J. E. Birren & Schaie, K. W. (Eds.), *Handbook of the psychology of aging.* N.Y.: Van Nostrand Reinhold Co.

Neugarten, B. L. 1968. *Middle age and aging*. Chicago, IL: University of Chicago Press.

Neugarten, B. L. 1969. Continuities and discontinuities of psychological issues into adult life. *Hum. Dev.*, **12**, 121–130.

Neugarten, B. L. 1970. Dynamics of transition of middle age to old age. *J. Geriatr. Psychiatry.* **4**, 1.

Neugarten, B. L. 1974. Age groups in American Society and the rise of the young-old. *Annals of Political and Social Sciences*, (Sept.).

Neugarten, B. L., & Moore, J. W. The changing age-status system. In B. Neugarten (Ed.). *Middle age and aging. A reader in social psychology.*

Newman, B., & Newman, P. 1979. *Development through life.* IL: The Dorsey Press.

Ornstein, P. 1968. The sorcerer's apprentice: The initial phase of training and education in psychiatry. Compr. Psychiatry, **9**(4), 293–315.

Osipow, S. H., Ashby, J. D., & Weul, H. W. 1966. Personality types and vocational choice: A test of Holland's theory. *Personnel and Guidance Journal*, **45**, 37–42.

Osipow, S. S. 1968. *Theories of career development*. Englewood Cliffs, N.J.: Prentice Hall.

Owen, R. 1974. *Middle age*. N.Y.: Columbia University Press.

Pardd, H., & Muter, R. (Eds.). 1963. *Dynamic Casework*. N.Y.: Family Serv. Assoc. of America.

Payne, P., Winter, D., & Bell, G. 1972. Effects of supervisor style on the learning of empathy in a supervision analogue. *Counselor Ed. and Supervision*, V. **II**, #4, June, pp. 262–267.

Perlman, G. 1972. Change in self and ideal self-concept congruence of beginning psychotherapist. *J. Clin. Pyschol.*, **28**, 404–408.

Pfeiffer, A. 1974. The difficulties of the training analyst in the training analysis. *Int. J. Psycholanal*, **55**, 79.

Rand, L. M., & Miller, A. L. 1972. A developmental cross sectioning of women's career and marriage attitudes and life plans. *J. Voc. Beh.*, 2, 317–331.

Raskin, D. Mini-boards: 1972. A means of evaluating psychiatric residents. Am. J. Psychiatry, 128(9), 1126.

Rebelsky. F. 1975. Life: The continuous process. N.Y.: Knopf.

Reik, T. 1948. Listening with the third ear.

Reigel, K. F. 1975. Adult life crisis: A dialectic interpretation of development. In *Life span developmental psychology*. N.Y.: Academic Press, Inc.

Rice, C., Alonso, A., Rutan, J. S. 1985. The fights of Spring: Separation, Individuation, and Grief in Training Centers. *Psychotherapy*, Spring, **22** (7), pp. 97–100.

Rioch, M., Coulter, W., & Weinberger, D. 1976. *Dialogues for therapists*. San Francisco, CA: Jossey-Bass.

Ripley, H., Johnson, M., & Scher, M. 1974. Evaluation of patient care when shared by medical students and resident psychiatrists. *J. Med. Educ.*, **49**, 245–253.

Rodlick, S., & Daniels, P. (Eds.) 1979. *Working it out*. Pantheon Books,

Roe, A. 1965. Changes in scientific activities with age. *Science*, **150**, 313–318.

Rogers, C. 1951. *Client centered therapy*. Boston, MA: Houghton Mifflin Co.

Rogers, K. 1976. The mid-career crisis. Sat. Rev. Soc., February, pp. 36–38.

Rosen, H. & Bartemeier, L. 1967. The psychiatric resident as participant therapist. *Am. J. Psychiatry*, **123** (11), 1371–1378.

Rosenblatt, A., & Mayer, J. 1975. Objectionable supervisory styles: Students' views. *Social Work*, pp. 184–89.

157

Russkin, F., & Rabiner, C. 1976. Psychotherapists' passivity—A major training problem. *Int. J. Psychoanal. Psychother.*, 5, 319–331.

Rusk, T. 1971. Psychiatric education in the emergency room setting. *Can. Psychiatr. Assoc. J.*, 16(2), 111–118.

Sachs, D., & Shapiro, S. 1974. Comments on teaching psychoanalytic psychotherapy in a residence training program *Psychoanal. Quart.* 43(1), 51–76.

Sachs, D., & Shaprio, S. 1976. On parallel process in therapy and teaching. *Psychoanal. Quarterly*, 45, 409–10.

Sachs, H., Henderson, M., & Bellis, E. 1968. Social worker participation in training residents in psychiatry. *Am. J. Orthopsychiatry*, 38(1), 25–30.

Salvendy, J. 1977. Education in psychotherapy: Challenges and pitfalls. *Can. Psychiat. Assoc. J.*, V. 22, pp. 435–440.

Sassen, G. 1977. Success Anxiety in women: A constructivist theory of its sources and significance. Unpublished manuscript, Harvard University.

Scanlan, J. 1972. Physician to student: The crisis of psychiatric residency training. *Am. J. Psychiatr.*, 12, 8–9.

Schaie, K. W., & Parham. 1974. Social responsibility in adulthood: Octogenetic sociocultural change. *J. Pers. Soc. Psychol.*, 30(4), 483–492.

Scherz. F. H. 1958. A concept of supervisor based on definitions of job responsibility. *Social Casework*, V. XXXIX, Oct. p. 435.

Schlessinger, N. 1966. Supervision of psychotherapy. *Arch. Gen. Psychiatry*, 15, 129–134.

Schuster, D., Sandt, J., & Thaler, O. 1972. *Clinical supervision of the psychiatric resident.* N.Y.: Bruner/Mazel, Inc.

Searles, H. F. 1955. The informational value of the supervisor's emotional experiences. *Psychiatry*, 18, 135–146.

Seiden, A. 1976. Overview: Research on the psychology of women. *Am. J. Psychiatry.* 133, 1111–1123.

Semrad, E. 1967. The organization of ego defenses and object loss. In D. M. Moriarty (Ed.), *The loss of loved ones.* Springfield, IL: Charles C. Thomas.

Semrad, E. 1969. *Teaching psychotherapy of psychotic patients.* N.Y.: Grune & Stratton.

Sheehy, G. 1974. *Passages.* N.Y.: E. P. Dutton, Inc.

Shershow, J., & Savodnik, I. 1976. Regression in the service of residency education. *Arch. Gen. Psychiatry.* October, pp. 1266–70.

Silberger, N. 1969. Supervision of psychotherapy. *Arch. Gen. Psychiatry*, 15, 128–134.

Simon, B. 1978. *Mind and madness in ancient Greece.* Ithaca, N.Y. and London: Cornell University Press.

Simon, R. 1974. On eclecticism. *Am. J. Psychiatry,* 131(2), 135–139.

Simpson, H., & McKinney, J. C. (Eds.). 1966. Social aspects of aging. Durham: Duke University Press.

Solnit, A. J. 1970, Learning from psychoanalytic supervision. *Int. J. Psychoanal.,* pp. 51–99.

Spreitzer, E., & Snyder, E. E. 1974. Correlates of life satisfaction among the aged. *J. Gerontol.,* 29(4), 454–458.

Suess, J. 1970. Self-confrontation of videotaped psychotherapy as a teaching device of psychiatric students. *J. Med. Educ.,* 45, 271–283.

Szasz, T. 1958. Psychoanalytic training: A socio-psychological analysis of its history and present status. *Int. J. Psychoanal.,* 39, 598–613.

Sze, W. 1975. *Human life cycle.* N.Y.: Jason Aronson.

Tarachow, S. 1963. An introduction to psychotherapy. N.Y.: International Universities Press, Inc.

Terman, L. M., & Oden, M. H. 1959. The gifted group at mid life. Stanford: Stanford University Press.

Titchener, J. 1968. "Observing psychotherapy: An experience in faculty resident relations." *Compr. Psychiatry,* 9(4), 392–399.

Towles, C. 1945. *Common human needs.* N.Y.: Basic Books.

Troll, L. 1975. *Early and middle adulthood,* Belmont Co.; Wadsworth's.

Truax, C. & Carkhuff, R. 1967. *Toward effective counseling and psychotherapy.* Chicago: Aldine Press.

Tyson, P. 1979. A conceptual model for a developmental approach to assessment, treatment planning and therapeutic intervention with children. Doctoral Dissertation, The Fielding Institute.

Vaillant, G. E. 1971. Theoretical hierarchy of adaptive ego mechanisms. *Arch. Gen. Psychiatry,* 24, 107–118.

Vaillant, G. E. 1974. Natural history of male psychological health II: Some antecedents of healthy adult adjustment. *Arch. Gen. Psychiatry,* 31, 15–22.

Vaillant, G. E. 1976. Natural history of male psychological health V: The relation of choice in ego mechanisms of defense to adult adjustment. *Arch. Gen. Psychiatry,* 33, 535–545.

Vaillant, G. E. 1977. *Adaptation to life.* Boston, MA: Little, Brown & Co.

Volkan, V. & Hawkins, D. 1972. The learning group. *Am. J. Psychiatry,* 128, 9.

Van Buskirk, D. 1979. Supervision in community mental health agencies. Read at *Conference on Supervision, Boston Institute for Psychotherapies, Inc., Oct.*

Van Gennep, A. 1908. *The rites of passage.* Chicago: The University of Chicago Press.

Walford, B. 1965. An immunological theory of aging. In R. Kastenbaum (Ed.), *Contributions to the psychology of aging.* N.Y.: Springer.

Waltzlawick, P. *et al.* 1967. *Pragmatics of Human Communication: A study of Interactional Patterns, Pathologies, and Paradoxes.* N.Y.: W. W. Norton.

Ward, N., & Stein, L. 1975. Reducing emotional distance: A new method to teach interviewing skills. *J. Med. Educ.* **50**, 605–614.

White, R. W. 1962. *Lives in progress.* N.Y.: Hall & Winston.

Wilensky, H. L. 1964. Varieties of work experience. In H. Borrow (Ed.), *Man in a world at work.* Boston: Houghton Mifflin Co.

Wilmer, H. 1968. Television as a participant recorder. *Am. J. Psychiatry,* **124**(9), 43–49.

Windholz, E. 1970. The theory of supervision in psychoanalytic education. *Int. J. Psychoanal.,* **51**, 593.

Winnicott, D. W. 1958. *Collected papers.* N.Y.: Basic Books.

Winnicott, D. S. 1969. *The child, the family, and the outside world,* Baltimore, MD: Penguin Books.

Winnicott, D. W. 1965. *The maturational processes and the facilitating environment.* London: Hogarth Press.

Winokur, G. & Cadoret, R. 1975. The irrelevance of menopause to depressive disease. In E. Sachar (Ed.), Topics in psychoendocrinology. N.Y.: Grune & Stratton.

Winstead, D., Bonovitz, J., Gale, M., & Evans, J. 1974. Resident peer supervision of psychotherapy. *Am. J. Psychiatry,* **131**,(3), 318–321.

Whitman, R., Kremer, M., & Baldridge, B. 1967. Experimental study of supervision of psychotherapy. *Am J. Psychiatry,* **4**, 427–431.

Woodmansey, A. 1979. The nurturing of medical students: A psychotherapeutic approach to psychiatric education. *Am. J. Psychotherapy,* **33**,(4), 583–591.

Yeats, E. 1979. Family rites of passage: A study of ritual and the school entry transition in five healthy families. Doctoral dissertation, University of Massachusetts.

Zilbach, J. *et al.* 1979. Reconsideration of aggression and self esteem in women. *Presentation at Int. Psychoanal. Assoc. Meeting, New York.*

Zilbach, J. *et al.* 1979. Family development and familial factors in etiology. In J. Noshpitz (Ed.), *Basic handbook of child psychiatry* (Vol. 2).

Index